Grace, Gratitude & Generosity
A FAMILY PORTRAIT

BY JANE MCBRIDE

FOREWORD BY HER DAUGHTER, STEPHANIE,
AND HER SON, CHRISTOPHER

EDITED BY SHEILA FRIEDECK, ASSOCIATE MANAGING EDITOR,
THE BEAUMONT ENTERPRISE

A PEDIMENT BOOK

For Joel

Published by Pediment Publishing, a division of The Pediment Group, Inc. www.pediment.com Printed in Canada

Acknowledgments

To my editors: Linda Gilchriest for that first freelance assignment; Ben Hansen for hiring me; Sheila Friedeck, who turned me into a columnist and stood behind me for 20 years; Ron Franscell, a gifted writer who fine-tuned my love of storytelling; Tim Kelly, who made this book possible; former publisher Aubrey Webb; publisher John Newhouse, who blessed this book project; and George Irish, retired president of Hearst Newspapers, for his quiet kindnesses. I am grateful beyond measure to each of you and the role you played in my career, and my life.

To my readers: You are the force behind this book. You take my words and, on a really good day, find something in them that speaks to your own life experiences. Thank you for the thousands of cards and letters and notes and phone calls, many of which kept me afloat in dark times. When you shared your joys and your sorrows with me, you reflected back what I strive to do - and one can't ask for much more than that.

To my writer friends, Rogayle Franklin, who started this all; Shari Fey, whose frank discussions broadened my horizons and made me a better reporter; to Elaine Wikstrom, who kept me honest; to the late Lela Davis, whose graceful example made me a better person; and to all the reporters and editors from whom I learned something each and every day.

To those who are in my core Enterprise group, who were there from the beginning and whose friendship I treasure – you know who you are and how much I love you.

To Pete Churton, an amazing photojournalist who patiently took my calls for help in getting photos together for the book – and the person I trusted to read behind me on the best stuff.

To Regina Rogers, who for the past 10 years never failed to greet me with "When are you going to publish a book?" OK, Regina, here it is.

To book editor Chris Fenison – thanks for taking my raw ideas and turning them into something better.

To my daughter, Stephanie, and my son, Chris, who endured untold embarrassment at my hands but always forgave me for exposing their lives to the world. Your love sustains me. To the rest of my family and friends, thanks for all the great material. You enrich my life. And to the love of my life, Joel, my husband of almost 30 years, a man who always believed I could do anything I set my mind to, and with infinite patience and love, finally made me believe it, too. Every day with you is a gift. I am a blessed woman.

Foreword

By Christopher & Stephanie

When Mother invited my sister and me to write a forward for her book, it seemed daunting. Mom has won countless awards for something that comes as natural to her as breathing. Truth is, it seems she needs to write almost as much as she needs to breathe.

I've written tons of things, from poetry to songs, but only my wife has been privy to my sophomoric ramblings and I've never been published. I've been content to leave that to professionals. I am, however, determined to give back this blessing in disguise. If nothing else, I hope to shed light on my mother's labor of love.

Understand that I'm a very private person and always have been, due to both my upbringing and being a veteran. Information in the military is handed out in a need-to-know basis. You don't need – you don't know. I've always told my mom that she can print whatever she feels, but at times it has put a strain on me.

I've had conversations that would, in other circumstances, seem like insanity. Friends asking me things like "So what do hard contacts taste like?" Even more embarrassing is the fact that all my family and friends now know that when I was a toddler I tried some douche powder. "No," the doctor told her when she called in a panic, "It won't hurt him . . . But he will have the sweetest breath in town."

There are rewards in having a columnist for a mother. I was a member of the local volunteer fire department when I was in high school and she wrote a story about the group. It seemed like a prime opportunity for embarrassment. One afternoon the volunteers met at the fire house and even had our pictures taken for the story. I'm here to tell you that for a week I was a celebrity for putting us in the paper. That's really saying something for a small farming community of a few hundred people.

There's also a down side to the limelight. I once had a boss who didn't have the same political views that my mom expressed and I had to look for work elsewhere. It wasn't my mom's fault that some people are sometimes too passionate about their views. Isn't that what makes this country great?

Now that I've poured out even more private information, I simply must admit one more thing. Through the good and bad I wouldn't have changed a thing. My sense of humor and privacy are still as intact as they need to be and most of what's happened because of the columns has enriched my life.

Thank you, Mother, for giving me a love of language, books, and a lust for self expression – no matter what the cost might be.

Christopher

"Gee, you look like your mother . . . you've even got the same crooked smile!"

It's true, genetics handed me the same smile that graces Mom's column each week. Mothers and daughters always share some physical characteristic, whether it's eyes or chin or even a laugh. We share more than that.

Boy, do we love our music. Put us in a room with hours to kill and a stack of old albums and we're as content as clams. Thanks to Mom, I grew up on an eclectic mix of Cat Stephens, Harry Chapin, Rita Coolidge, Jackson Browne, Joan Baez, Bob Dylan and Emmy Lou Harris. She endured my years of Duran-Duran and Flock of Seagulls until I eventually found my way back to the good stuff.

In many ways, Mom and I are polar opposites. Once, at a dinner party, it came up that I was her daughter. My friend, who once worked with her, loudly exclaimed "No way! You're so Sarah Jessica Parker and your mom is so, so . . . Emmy Lou Harris!!"

While I'm insanely jealous that my mom got to be Emmy Lou, it's true that Mother will play guitar in her garden clogs whereas I'll unashamedly dance in stilettos, thank you very much.

Quite often, I meet people who simply adore my mother. I've known someone for many months before he or she makes the connection that I am "Jane McBride's Daughter." Recently, Mom and I had dinner. An acquaintance called me over to say hello. When Mom came up behind me, he looked at her, looked at me and said, "Stephanie, you are a wonderful and charming person in your own right, but that's nothing compared to the fact you are Jane McBride's daughter!" As a teenager I used to find this embarrassing. As an adult it's become a great moment of pride.

As I've matured, I've realized how much I actually am like Dear Old Mom. Not only do we look more alike than ever, but there are moments when we discover some freakish shared trait (not be revealed here). We look at each other, laughing, and repeat . . . "Mirror, Mirror, on the wall, I am my mother after all." Our laughter acknowledges that internal horror every woman has of learning the things that drive her crazy about her mother are now a part of her.

The relationship I have with my mother is a strong one, but bears moments of fragility. The irony, I believe, is that any difficulties my mom and I have are due to the complex relationship she had with her own mother. The unresolved issues of their relationship sometimes carry over into ours.

Now that I am the mother of the two most beautiful boys who ever existed, I am overwhelmed by the intensity of love I feel. I am fiercely protective of my boys and would do anything for them. It occurred to me that this is the love my mom feels. I think of her litany of questions. "Did you lock your doors?" and "Is your security system on?" As much as it drives me crazy, I now realize it's driven by the same parental love I feel for my kids.

Many people have been affected by Mom's ability to touch them through her writing. Who knew the black and white of words on newsprint could tug at your emotions the way Mother's do?

I have cried and laughed through many of her stories, as you have. As a private person, there has been a certain amount of discomfort at being the subject of some of them, but no one could be more proud of what she has accomplished.

I've watched as people have embraced my mother and sent her countless thank you cards and letters. I am very proud of her, but for reasons other than her gifted writing abilities.

She is one of the most humble, genuine and caring people I know. The generosity she extends to others is simply remarkable.

Through the years my mom has become The Person I Wish to Emulate. Mirror, Mirror, on the Wall . . .

Stephanie

Table of Contents

Preface

"Where's Janie?"

"Oh, she's off somewhere with her nose in a book."

During my Arkansas farm family childhood, while my cousins were out playing, I was lost in a world of words that transported me beyond the insular boundaries of my life. My grandmother never got past the sixth grade but read the newspaper and the Bible daily. My mother, one of eight children, loved learning and was the first to graduate from high school, despite working along with her siblings to keep the family fed. My dad was named after his father's favorite author, Zane Grey.

Books were a luxury for us. The first ones I read came from the school library. My grandmother raised me, and she couldn't drive. But during the summer, she would convince my stern grandfather to make a stop at the public library when we went to town for supplies. The little library had a three-book maximum, but the librarian, seeing my hunger for reading, allowed me to stock up on as many as I thought I could read before we came back. I went through everything in the library that looked even remotely interesting.

Besides being The Bookworm and The Tomboy, I was the tallest, skinniest, shiest kid in the class. I was in the odd position of having 7 brothers and sisters but growing up an only child after my aunts and uncles married and moved away from my grandparents' home.

After high school, I moved to Texas to go to college, but got married at 19 instead and became a mother at 20. The marriage disintegrated. I entered the work world, serving food at Luby's

Cafeteria, working in a camera shop, in the medical field, in office management and property management.

And always, I kept reading. I was in my 30s before I had a chance to go to college and take some creative writing classes. I joined the Golden Triangle Writer's Guild, worked on the mechanics of writing with a critique group and got a shot at freelancing for The Beaumont Enterprise, a Hearst daily newspaper with a history of being a training ground for writers who went on to memorable careers. I loved it from day one, though after they hired me full time (Praise the Lord!), I kept waiting for someone to tell me they'd made a mistake and kick me out the door. I was lucky to have some great editors who saw promise in me, respected my voice and gave me a place to use it.

I've written thousands of feature stories, plus a good number of news and 1A stories where I was a bystander reporting the facts. As much as I loved being able to craft those pieces, it has been the column that has been my heart. It is there that I could share myself.

And boy, did I share. Linda Weltner, a columnist whose work I admired, once said she had to fight with editors who thought she was too open in her columns, especially about her shortcomings and failures, something that might put off some readers. Weltner replied that she was willing to lay it all on the line because she didn't want to be a coward.

I understand that. If you are going to write a personal column, how can you not get personal? Anything less is dishonest.

I've written about being born a "bastard;" about being molested by an alcoholic uncle, about the burdensome lack of confidence, insecurities and selfishness of youth that kept me from being a better wife and the kind of mother my kids deserved; about being diagnosed with breast cancer and the treatment that followed.

As much of a downer as that sounds, my column always been about the amazing power of the human spirit. I believe in the power of love –

and I believe there is far more good in the world than evil – and that it is up to us to foster that good with all we have in us.

And lest you get the wrong idea, for the record, I wrote probably as many humor columns as serious ones. A good laugh is far more satisfying than a frown.

Now, 20 years after joining the world of journalism, I have retired from The Enterprise, though I still write the column once known as Just Plain Jane. It has been the love of my work life, something I believe I was meant to do, though God sure took his time getting me there. OK, fine, maybe it was me who dragged my feet.

I leave you with this. As my favorite columnist Sharon Randall said in the preface to her book, "Birdbaths and Paper Cranes," we are far more alike than we are different in matters of the heart.

You hold in your hands a diary of sorts, written about a private life for public view, in hopes that those shared life experiences double your joys and triumphs and halve your sorrows. I hope you find something of value here, and that your life be filled with grace, gratitude and generosity.

Jane McBride
Author

Section One

June 19, 1992 to December 10, 1993

Mom and Dad
(Juanita Nowlin Swann and Zane Thomas Burr)

Finding my father

June 19, 1992

I saw him before he saw me.

He paced beneath a metal carport, as uncomfortable as the faded brown knit tie that hadn't seen daylight for years. He wore a short-sleeved shirt, freshly pressed. His squeaky-new department store shoes and the tweed hat he twisted impatiently gave him away.

The too-thin, lanky man carried more than his hat in his hands. He carried his heart, and as I savored the first look I'd had of my dad, I felt my own break. The image conveyed all the emotions, all the baggage that accompany the delayed coming together of parent and adult child.

I'd found my dad two weeks before, living in a small town in Arkansas less than an hour's drive from where I grew up. I drove up to meet him. I liked the idea of seeing him for the first time in his element, surrounded by the things that would tell me who this man is. We Southerners are such products of our history that I longed to get a glimpse of his.

For years, the strongest emotional tie to my father was fear. Fear that I would never find or know him. Fear that if I did, he would reject me. Fear that he would turn out to be a man I could not respect.

My insecurities created a need to have a father of whom I could be proud. Not success or money, but goodness, kindness, character and integrity – things I sought in my own life.

I believe God brings things to us in his own time and for his own reasons. I sense several lessons in the gift of my father, not the least of which is acceptance.

How presumptuous of me to lay out a host of requirements. To say, "OK, God, here is 'Jane's Dad.' "

My father is far from perfect. A former juke joint musician, he lived too hard and drank too much for too many years. But he also is loving, smart, funny and sensitive. He fearlessly races through life with laughter as his calling card.

He is who he is, and he offers me unconditional love.

The days we spent together yielded many gifts. Dad and I share more than the Burr bloodline. We love the outdoors, bird watching and dill pickles. From the day we learned to read, we have been word struck, lost in our own worlds.

Although my birth certificate didn't reflect it, I carried his name. Change one letter in his first name, Zane, and you have mine.

He, too, knew the emptiness of father hunger. He lost his dad when he was 10. His favorite memory is sitting in his dad's lap, soaring above the forests and deltas in a tiny plane. Dad's single-engine Aeronica hasn't left the ground for years. It's lovingly hangered, waiting for my brothers, Carl and David, to continue the tradition.

I will never meet my feisty grandmother or my Uncle Aaron, the tall gentle man who sat on the front porch and played the guitar while my father played the fiddle. I can't – won't – dwell on the things I missed. It is enough to look at the photographs and drink in second-hand memories through the stories Dad so loves to tell.

I'm far too grateful for the memories we will build together.

On that first visit, I spent hours walking the peaceful deep woods where my dad lives on the land that has been in his – in our – family for at least four generations. I felt that peace transfer to me as surely as I felt the inexplicable ties to those whose blood I share.

I felt the void that had far too much with shaping my life slowly fill up. No one ever again can deny my heritage. I know who I am and to whom I belong.

At home, on the antique secretary that holds my favorite books and other treasures, a flowery, sentimental Easter card holds center court. It isn't the verse or the occasion that keeps it displayed long past the holiday.

It is the signature, written in an elegant hand that says simply, "Love, Dad."

ME AND DAD THE DAY WE MET TAKEN IN FRONT
OF THE ORIGINAL LOG CABIN OF MY GREAT-
GREAT-GRANDFATHER, DANIEL CHANCE. FIVE
GENERATIONS OF DAD'S FAMILY (CHANCE/BURR)
HAVE LIVED ON THE LAND

Letting go never is easy
Feb 19, 1993

I loved her the moment I saw her, that afternoon 11 years ago when Hubby came home with a big grin and said, "I've got a surprise for you."

As he bent down, a fluffy puppy tumbled from his arms and straight into my heart.

He found Nikki keeping her brothers and sisters company in a cardboard box beside the highway. "Free Puppies," the box proclaimed.

I was dogless at the time, which is rare. During my lifetime, I've had a Collie, a Cocker Spaniel, and Irish Setter, a black Lab, two Schnauzers and various unknowns.

Hubby knew I wanted a big, outside dog to run and play with and give bear hugs. As a Lab/Shepherd mix, he figured Nikki would meet my needs.

Nikki settled into our lives in a quiet, unassuming way. She had impeccable manners, a tender spirit and gentle demeanor. When Nikki wanted something, she asked politely, never demanding.

The closest she came to being pushy was when she needed a hug. She would wait until I sat down and slowly work her way into my lap, sitting erect, facing one side so she could lean against my chest.

Nikki grew quickly. It wasn't long until her head began to touch my chin, then rest on my shoulder. Soon, she had to back up and lower herself gradually, since she was taller than my seated self. It was a funny sight from the front, a big yellow dog and my arms and legs.

She couldn't comfortably stay that way long, but there were days when she just seemed to need my lap.

Five years later, when I gave Hubby a Schnauzer for our anniversary, Nikki didn't mind. She who loved indiscriminately was excited about having a playmate. Unfortunately, J.J. had other ideas. She quickly claimed the house as her territory and let Nikki know she was boss.

You'd think Nikki would let J.J. know she had been there longer, while J.J. was merely a Johnnie-come-lately. But that was never Nikki's style.

When our third dog, Orphan Annie was dumped unannounced into our yard this past year, Nikki welcomed her, too. She became the playmate J.J. had refused to be. Nikki had a hard time keeping up with Annie, who is 1,000 pounds of energy packed into a 25-pound body. When Nikki tired, Annie would merely continue to run and leap and use Nikki for a springboard. Nikki took it all in good humor, the way she did everything else.

After the kids grew up and moved away, I spent less time than I should have with Nikki. There were days when all she got was a quick ear-scratching as she walked me to the door. She never chastised me. In her placid way, she'd wag her tail, give me a quick kiss and lumber back to lie down.

This past Saturday, I got up early and spent a couple of hours with Nikki. I sat on the deck beside her, rubbed her favorite spots and we had a good, long talk. For the first time in years, Nikki slowly and awkwardly climbed into my lap and leaned heavily against me.

All I could do was bury my face in her chest and sob, knowing it was the last time I would ever hold her that way. Nikki's heart, so generous and full of love, was giving out.

No matter how much we loved Nikki, we knew it was wrong to ask her to live with pain just because we didn't want to make a difficult decision. After talking with our vet, we knew we had to let her go.

Nikki and I shared breakfast, then went for a walk to get the paper. An hour later, we put her in the back of the truck and my husband rode with her while I drove to the vet. It was his chance to have a few private minutes to tell her goodbye in his own way.

Our vet is one of those special people who understands the bonds we make with our pets. He never rushed us, giving us time to come to terms with letting her go. He and his wife, tears streaming down her face, stood quietly as I nuzzled her one last time, told her how much I loved her and what a good friend she had been.

For the past week, in an unexplainable development, my wild Annie has changed personalities. She is markedly quieter, calmer and has even started gaining some manners. It is almost as if she knows it's up to her to take Nikki's place.

This weekend, I'm going to plant some wildflowers on Nikki's grave, tell her what a good job she did raising Annie, and tell her not to worry. She came first.

Tell me about the woman you know
March 19, 1993

She was born 66 years ago today, the fourth child of eight in a tiny farm town in Arkansas. From the beginning, she was smart and sassy, quick to laughter and quick with words.

She grew from a tow-headed girl to a young woman with a head full of dark, untamed hair that curled around a lovely face, with a peaches-and-cream complexion dusted with just enough freckles to keep her honest.

She worked hard in the fields and in the home to help her family through tough times. There were years when a crop was all that kept the family from going hungry. There was the year her father was in a tuberculosis hospital and she and her brothers and sisters had to take up the slack. Tough times were something she would know all too well during her life.

She is my mother, and I want to talk about her in a way we never could face to face.

When I was born, I was sick a lot and Mother didn't have the means to take care of me. She moved to Texas and my grandparents raised me, so I never knew her well. I never really knew her at all.

A relationship takes time to build. You don't forge a strong bond by spending a few days a year with each other. You don't have the day-to-day experiences that draw you close.

Mother and I never had the luxury of getting to know each other the way we should. It is only now, when I have grown children of my own, that I am beginning to know her, even a little.

I think I inherited several things from Mother that surely must have been through genes, since environmental factors didn't apply in our case. Mother gave me her chin, her blue/green eyes, her hips (Thank you very much, Mother) and according to my husband, her stubbornness in thinking I am always right.

I, however, disagree, and know I am right about this.

Most of all, she gave me life.

This week, in anticipation of her birthday, I called a couple of her sisters and asked them to help me see her through eyes other than my own.

Aunt Shirley said she can't remember that much about Mother as a young woman - except that she was beautiful - but she remembers very clearly the day I was born at home, in a little house just across the railroad tracks from her.

"In those days, pregnancy and giving birth were very hush-hush. I remember everyone was running around, going in and out and they thought they were pulling one over on me, but I knew what was going on." She said. "They just thought they had me fooled."

Aunt Gladys, four years younger than Mother, was perhaps closer to her than any of the others.

"We all were close," she adds. "I remember when I was 11 or 12. Daddy had started a cotton crop and after school we walked to the fields to work. Me and your Aunt Sue would stop and play and your mother would try to get us to come on and pick cotton and do right. She always did what she was told. We'd be playing on top of the cotton, but she was out there working."

My favorite view of my mother as a young woman comes from my dad.

Dad says he loved Mother from the day he first saw her. He remembers most her zest for life. Through his eyes, I see her then - as beautiful and untamed as the old-fashioned roses that run first one way, then the other, with thorns every so often to protect them.

Her eyes said it all, Dad recalled. They burned with mischief and passion and a desire to know everything about life, traits he knew all too well.

How could he not have loved her?

My relationship with my mother has been a rocky one. We've never really learned how to talk to each other. We always seem to be on guard and I know I'm more comfortable holding something back, afraid of what might happen if I let her in too close.

But we are trying.

It is comforting to me to understand, after all these years, that she loves me.

Happy birthday, Mother. I love you, too.

Dented love

Oct. 1, 1993

My son has a new love in his life.

Chris recently completed his Army service and is living with us while he gets back on his feet. Because he sold his truck when he enlisted, he had to find a new vehicle. It was harder than we expected. Everything he looked at was either out of his price range or a piece of junk.

In a wonderful stroke of luck (and divine intervention), he found a beautiful, classic 1978 Ford LTD with one owner (we knew her) who took excellent care of the car. The inside was immaculate and the air conditioner blew frigid air (his first air-conditioned car).

It was very blue and very, very big.

When my 6-food 5-inch son climbed into the trunk to check some wiring, he could stretch his legs all the way across the car.

When his girlfriend came over, she took one look at the car and said, "Chris. It's you."

And it is. Chris has always preferred classics to newer models. He's always preferred something just a little bit different, from clothes to music to cars.

He affectionately dubbed the car The Blue Blimp and has been taking great care of it, keeping it clean and waxing it until it shines.

Recently, I got up one foggy morning and, still in a fog myself, absentmindedly backed out of the driveway.

I felt the car shudder and heard a thud. My stomach sank.

The Blue Blimp.

I got out and forced myself to look. There was a big, concave dip in the front fender. As I stood there, a little chunk of rusty metal fell from underneath the fender with a pitiful plunk!

I gathered up my courage, went inside and knocked on my son's door.

"Come in," he mumbled.

"He was lying on his stomach, face turned to the wall, eyes closed. I sat on the side of the bed and started rubbing his shoulder.

"Before I tell you what I have to say, I just want you to remember I have loved and taken care of you for 22 years," I began.

"What did I do?" he mumbled, still half asleep.

"Nothing. It's what I did. I . . . bumped into your car." (I figured bumped had a gentler connotation that crashed.)

He let out a low and very painful groan and threw the covers over his head.

"How bad is it? This muffled weak, voice asked.

"Well," I hesitated.

Is it a little crease or is it completely crumpled?"

"It's a pretty big dent," I said. "And it has these long, white scratches where it took the paint off."

He was quiet for just a moment, but long enough for me to imagine how he must feel and dread what he was about to say.

"I'm sorry, Chris," I offered.

"Mom, don't worry about it. It's OK."

"No, it's not OK. I feel awful."

He rolled over, opened his eyes and looked at me.

"Mom, if I know you, you've been sitting out there by yourself for 15 minutes, crying and all upset because you feel so bad. Then, you had to come wake me up and tell me. I certainly don't want to add anything to that. You feel bad enough as it is."

"I do. I feel awful," I agreed.

"Don't sweat it," he said. "It's already got some road scars," he added, trying to console me. "If you can pop the fender back out, I'll pay to have it painted," I offered.

"Mom, I'm not going to soak you for a paint job because you dented the fender," he said.

"No. I want to do it," I told him.

"Look, I know you need to get to work, so don't worry about it. It's fine," he said, then rolled over to go back to sleep.

On the way to work, I got to thinking about how I would have reacted if the tables were turned. If he had hit my car, I don't know if I could have been as generous.

Yes, I would be aware how awful he would feel and how hard it would be to tell me. I would reassure him it was going to be all right, but before I got to that stage, I can almost promise you I would have said something like, "Chris, I can't believe you were so careless," or "Didn't you even look?"

I guess at least one of us has our priorities straight.

Letters reveal inner feelings
Oct. 29, 1993

Letter writing might be a dying art, but thank heavens it isn't dead yet.

I don't think I've ever gotten a letter from a friend or relative that I didn't re-read at least once. Many of them I read several times over as I answer them, since the best letters keep a running commentary.

I have a letter from my grandmother (the guiding light in my life for 21, too-short years) written when I was 8, encouraging me through the trauma of a tonsillectomy.

I have a letter from my brother, Johnny, written at least 10 years ago when he was in the Navy. It contains lyrics from a song he loved at the time and is quite introspective, sharing thoughts of that stage in his life.

I have a letter from my sister, Gloria, when she was in the Navy. It gives vivid descriptions of how she spent her days in boot camp. As often the case with Gloria, it is brave and upbeat on the surface but the loneliness of a young woman a couple of thousand miles from home clearly comes through.

A letter from my sister, Billie, written in 1963, is full of teen-age passion for the Beatles. Billie later went to New Orleans to see them in person. There will be a column to come about that experience. Trust me. It was a doozie.

I have every letter my husband ever wrote me. I wouldn't take a million dollars for them (even if he begged me to reconsider, and believe me, he would). When I found my father two years ago- and discovered two new brothers and a sister- I got to know one of my brothers through his letters.

My brother Carl is a verbal person more than a writer, so we first met on the phone and later, we had long conversations in person. We discovered we share many interests and philosophies and parts of our lives have taken similar paths. My Dad isn't a letter writer, either. Cards and a note are about the most I'll get from him in writing.

My brother David, on the other hand, is a fabulous letter writer. His introductory letter gave me insight into what kind of man he is – bright, thoughtful, opinionated (like me) and with a deliciously weird and wonderful sense of humor.

I cherish Dave's letters. They make me laugh and they've made me cry. If he ever chooses a second career, he could do well as a wordsmith. His letters caught me up on the 40 years I missed with him and – at their very best – gave me glimpses into his heart.

Letters from Gladys, my friend of 20 years, are numbered among my favorite. I have letters when she moved to Houston about 15 years ago, letters from Saudi Arabia when she and her husband lived there and letters from California, where she now lives.

The letters kept me informed about her life and gave me emotional support in tough times, as mine have to her. They reassure me that she is happy and doing well and remind me that our friendship can't be broken by physical distance.

When I re-read Gladys' letters, I remember her divorce and relocation to start a new life. Other letters describe the joy of finding Michael – her heartmate, husband and life's partner – their marriage and the difficulty in being a modern, career woman living in the restrictive atmosphere of Saudi Arabia.

Her letters of the past few years detail living with Thea, Roni and Lexi, her three sensitive, independent and high-spirited daughters. I can just feel the hormones careening through that house.

That's why I love letters. Letters are a chronicle of our lives at that exact moment in time when we put pen to paper. Our lives change. We change. But our pasts shape our futures.

I think Gladys put it best in her most recent letter to me.

"I think about you a lot. I came in to the office a few days ago and flipped on the radio to the sounds of Handel's Water Music and traveled back over the years to you and Janie (her sister) and everyone and everything. Isn't it nice how time has rewritten every line, except the very best stuff? I miss you."

I miss you, too, Glad. Keep those letters coming.

Lucky 13
Dec. 10, 1993

In three days, my husband and I will celebrate our 13th wedding anniversary. It is a special year for us since we were married on the 13th of the month.

The day I married my husband was one of the luckiest days of my life.

It's hard to believe it's been that long. It seems like just yesterday when he walked into a room and caught my eye. At 6 feet 5 inches, with blue eyes, blond hair, a red beard and a contagious Irish grin, he was easy on the eyes and hard to miss.

I like tall. Being 5 feet 10 inches, it takes a tall man to whirl me comfortably around a dance floor, to kiss the top of my head in a moment of affection and to make me feel dainty and feminine when he chastises me and says, "Wait a minute, now, Missy."

During the 13 years we've been married, I've learned a lot from, and about the man who can still make my heart flutter with a sweet word and a smile.

I learned his heart needs as much love as mine does. Affection is the food of his life, and he has a huge appetite. He would rather I beat him up (like I could!) than withhold a hug. It is a very rare day indeed, that he doesn't tell me he loves me and that we don't fall asleep at night with our arms around each other.

I also learned how to fight.

My husband is Irish all the way. He was raised in a family that says what they think, when they think it. That goes double when their dander is up.

I, on the other hand, usually avoid confrontation at all costs. During the first year of our marriage, when we would disagree, he would have his say and I would clam up. He would be ready for a good air-cleaning and I would simply leave the room.

Not for long, because he wouldn't allow it. He'd follow me and refuse to let it go until I spoke back. It took years, but when I finally did let go (something you do not want to be a witness to, let alone on the receiving end of – trust me) he stood there while I gave it my best shot, then burst into laughter.

"Now, don't you feel better?" he asked placidly.

It took days for my blood pressure to come down.

He taught me what faith in someone can do. I tend to lapse into periods of self-doubt. Because I drive myself hard toward achievement, I fear failure.

No matter what the goal, he believes I can attain it. He works hard at building my confidence. He is my biggest supporter and most ardent fan and woe be unto him who criticizes me.

He encourages me to be the best I can be. He is not the type of man to be threatened by others' successes. In fact, there is very little he IS threatened by. When we shop, he carries my purse to free up my hands. As a joke, he once sauntered into the living room wearing my flowered robe. Yep, this man is secure in his masculinity.

Being married to a newspaper columnist leaves him vulnerable. Because he is such a huge part of my life, he's often the subject of my musing and he takes it in stride.

In the beginning, I referred to him only as Hubby in my columns, thinking he deserves at least a shred of privacy from the people who don't thrust my column at him (laughing delightedly) on those weeks it's about him. At his office, he good-naturedly answers to Hubby, Mr. Jane or any other nickname they throw his way.

I've learned the power of trust. I trust him with my heart and with my life, and I know that he does the same. I know I come first with him.

Everything he does that would affect me, even a little, every decision he makes that concerns us, is made with me in mind.

I've learned the importance of accepting the fact that all human beings – including spouses and children – are less than perfect. I've learned that in day-to-day life, we are going to wound each other. I've learned the importance of forgiving and forgetting those hurts.

And I've learned why God gave my husband such a big body. He needed the space to hold his bigger-than-life personality and, most of all, his huge heart.

Section Two

February 11, 1994 to September 21, 1997

THE SWANN FAMILY (MOM, GLORIA, BILLIE,
ANITA, CHARLES, JOHN, JUDY, SUSAN)

Sprint across field immortalizes fan

Feb. 11, 1994

*I*t was 1964. Like millions of her peers, 15-year-old Billie Jean was madly, hopelessly in love with four irreverent young men from Liverpool badly in need of haircuts.

My sister was the ultimate Beatlemaniac. She had every record, knew the lyrics to every song, spoke the lingo (gear, fab) listened faithfully to Murray the K and her room was a veritable shrine.

She had Beatles dolls, magazines and a color photo of each Beatle with a gum wrapper chain she'd painstakingly made of their exact height, hanging next to each photo.

When she heard they were coming to New Orleans, she'd written for concert tickets, using money she had earned working after school and on weekends. There was one hurdle – convincing Mother to let her go. Just in case, she had a contingency plan. Billie, the model student and dutiful daughter who always did what was expected, would simply call a cab, wait for it on the porch of a vacant house a few doors down, and run away from home.

Luckily, they agreed to let our 19-year-old sister, Gloria take her on the bus.

She arrived at night, awed by the lights and bustle and trembling with anticipation of everything she was about to see.

At Tulane Stadium, Billie and Gloria were seated half way up. Billie was transfixed, transported. Near the end of the program, caught up in the incredible sweep of emotions the Beatles evoked in their fans, Billie lost it.

She looked across the field and realized there was nothing between her and the Fab Four but a railing, a 5-foot-drop and yards of field. She went for it.

"It was so strange. It was just, I must be down there with them. They were playing, 'I Want To Hold Your Hand' and I said, Well, I've got to go now."

She vaulted over the rail, dropped to the ground and ran. Gloria, well aware what might happen if she returned home minus one little sister ("Well, gee, Mother. It's kind of hard to explain…") leaned over the rail and enlisted the help of one of the cops on horseback working security.

"That's my sister," she screamed, pointing to Billie, who was at warp speed by that time, "Get my sister!"

Billie, surrounded by throngs of maniacal teen-age girls, took advantage of her diminutive stature.

"By this time, there were probably 1,000 kids on the field. The police formed a cordon, gathered them up and were sweeping them to the end of the field. I was so little I ducked down and scurried between people's legs."

She saw nothing but open field and nothing slowed her down, until the lone cop dismounted and said, "Your sister's waiting for you over there, Dear."

There Billie stood, still half a football field away, slightly dazed, muddy, sans one shoe, sporting a torn skirt and a broken heart.

"They hoisted me back up, pushed me over the rail and told Gloria, 'Here you go, Ma'am.' By that time I was in tears, crushed that I hadn't gotten closer, but so excited that I had gotten on the field, while there were so many who never even tried."

Billie and Gloria left the stadium. A long, black limo pulled up. A horde of screaming fans surged forward, carrying her with them. Billie found herself wedged nose to nose- through the windowpane, of course – with John, Paul, George and Ringo.

"I'm slobbering on the glass, crying, Paul! Paul!" she says. "I can hear Gloria behind me, saying, 'Oh, my God, oh my God,' sure that I was about to be swept away under the limo. It was a wonderful moment."

They walked around New Orleans and listened to the jazz floating on the sultry, night air. They ended up at Café Du Monde, where their waiter took one look at Billie- in her agitated state of disarray- and informed her that the Beatles had been there that very afternoon and had sat at the very same table and had used, yes, that very same sugar bowl.

"I dug through both our purses until I found a container and filled it with sugar. I kept it for years," she says.

The next day, Billie was the hit of PN-G High School. The president of the local Beatles fan club, Susan Ketcherside, told Billie her sprint and abduction by the lone cop had been shown on TV.

She had seen the Beatles. She had screamed and cried herself voiceless. In fact she says, her voice has never been quite the same.

Or her life.

She loves you, yeah, yeah, yeah…

Yeah.

Time, love help broken hearts mend
March 18, 1994

I lost my grandmother 26 years ago. It was 10 years after her death before I could talk about it without crying. At times, I thought I had died with her - that I was only a body walking around, a hollow shell that had lost its heart and soul.

My grandmother raised me, loved, nurtured and protected me. I moved away from her Arkansas home after high school. As a young wife, I was too busy learning about life and too self-absorbed to answer her letters regularly or make more than infrequent five-hour trips home to visit.

Three years later, she was gone.

The great sadness of my life is that I never got to share my adulthood with her. I never got to tell her how much I learned from her and what she meant to me, to ask about her childhood, or to discuss the meaning of life.

As my grandmother lay dying of lung cancer at home, as she had wanted, her eight children and numerous grandchildren gathered around her. The last month of her life, one of them sat beside her bed and held her hand every moment of every hour. One of her sons-in-law took time off work to be with her. She was the light of so many lives.

There were minutes when she was lucid, and long hours when she was not. At one point, she told me that she was ready to go. The only thing stopping her was knowing she was leaving her children – whom she loved so much – behind. I was barely able to choke out, "I love you."

Even though I was able to tell her that, it didn't seem to be enough. For months after her death, I drowned in guilt. Why didn't I answer her letters? Why hadn't I done more to show her how much I appreciated the sacrifices she had made? Why hadn't I made time to be with her?

One night, as I lay in bed, heartsick, my grandmother appeared to me. She stood at the foot of the bed, a hazy presence that I felt more than saw.

Although she didn't speak, the meaning of her words coursed through my entire body as clearly as if they had been spoken – "It's OK. I know you love me. It's going to be all right."

I firmly believe that she felt my pain. She didn't want me to feel guilty and found a way to bring me the message that our bond was strong enough that death couldn't break it. The peace I hadn't been able to find on my own settled over me, brought by her loving heart.

Years later I began to understand that even if we tell our loved ones a million times a day, "I love you," it isn't enough to save us from guilt and regret. There will always be something else we wish we had done. It is a part of the grieving process that we can't escape.

My grandmother didn't have to hear, "I love you," to know it. We had 20 years of shared, daily experiences that love built. She knew her presence in my life and in my heart.

Our friends lost their son this past week in a tragic accident. There was no time to prepare, to say a final, "I love you," or "Good-bye."

Those of us who know and love them are numb with empathy. Our own hearts break for them, even as we realize those of us who haven't lost a child can't imagine the depth of the grief they must feel.

It's hard to know how to help. Grief is a private thing that each person must endure in his or her own way. Some of us need others around us, need to talk about our loss and remember our loved one in conversations that help us heal.

Others need to be alone. In those early stages, the pain is too raw. We are unwilling and unable to share our feelings with others. We retreat and turn to our mates, or our parents, our siblings, to those closest to us who most clearly understand how we feel.

So, despite our fears that we will say the wrong thing or make an unwelcome intrusion, the rest of us do what we can. We love them, put them in our prayers and try to be there if and when they need us.

It takes time to heal.

Survivors grow to understand we did what we could, as best we could. If the situation were reversed, we wouldn't want the loved ones we leave behind to blame themselves or feel guilty. So we try our best to do what we would ask of them.

I cherish the 20 years I had with my grandmother. As I live my life, I offer thanks for the role she played in it. I am comforted by the knowledge that when something significant happens to me, she either celebrates – or weeps – with me.

And I look forward to the day when we can sit and talk – woman to woman – for as long as we want.

Men and power tools
Aug. 26, 1994

If I ever decide to begin a new career, I know exactly what it will be. I want to study anthromanpology.

OK. Maybe there is no such thing as anthromanpology, but there sure ought to be. If anthropology is supposed to be the science of man, why are we wasting so much time on both genders? We women aren't hard to figure out. Just ask us what we want and we'll tell you. In detail.

It's men who are so confusing. And if you ask them what it is they really want, you'll get a one-word answer. A one-syllable, one-word answer.

And I want to know why – when you promise at the altar to love, honor and cherish us for the rest of our lives, you forget this the first time we have some chore for you to do around the house?

I don't recall any phrase in the marriage vow that says: "Except when it comes to any task involving power tools that is for the specific benefit of the woman of the house only."

There is a dichotomy here that perplexes me to no end. Men LOVE power tools. If you want to get them out of the Barcalounger, just confiscate the remote control (you might want to slip a tranquilizer into their morning coffee first) and tell them you need something from the hardware store.

Men LOVE hardware stores. They can spend hours walking up and down the aisles, checking the fine print on boxes for the horsepower or watts or mega whatever measurement of power a tool has.

They will congregate and exchange such information as, "Yeah, I find if you want to do the job right, you'll need at least one million, eight-hundred thousand, five hundred and sixty-four watts on this baby."

So why, given their natural attachment to manly tools, do they resist simple projects in the kitchen, bathroom, or bedroom? Give them a chore involving the garage or one that requires blueprints, a truckload of lumber or concrete and they're thrilled. Yeah, you can almost hear them growl, this is job for a REAL man.

But ask them to make one little shelf for the pantry or hang one little light over the sewing machine or – God forbid – repair something that's broken, and they suddenly find some pressing problem that must be solved.

"I'll look at it later," they promise. Later never comes.

The one exception is the strange and bizarre behavior that comes over them when they encounter a woman in need –not of their household. If their neighbor's or friend's wife needs something done, our gentlemanly, chivalrous spouses jump to the rescue.

"No problem, Missy. I'll have this fixed for you in no time."

When my husband needed help rebuilding our front porch, at least four of our friends visited at various times and jumped right in. There they were, in the heat, sweating up a storm while doing some heavy labor.

Believe me, we appreciated it. But also believe me when I tell you I'd bet you a dollar to a doughnut their wives were at home tripping over broken chairs in a dark pantry or sweating under a broken ceiling fan – and cussing up a storm.

I think I know how to solve this problem.

We've got grandparents day and secretaries day and bosses day and you-name-it day, so why can't we have wives day?

I say we get a group of our married friends together – five will do – and each wife will pick out a chore she's been waiting for her husband to do for four or five years. That shouldn't be hard.

Then, the husbands will take turns going around to the houses – one day spent at each – taking care of those chores. Each husband will be excused from working at his own home.

Everybody wins.

The men can flex their muscles and rev up power tools and stretch out extension cords and engage in some real male bonding. Mission accomplished, they can bask in the adoring light of the appreciative wives' smiles.

And when they go home, they will find a wife who is in a decidedly better frame of mind.

One who might even dig the remote control out of the trash can.

It's your turn, Son
Oct. 14, 1994

My son Christopher turned 24 this week.

I asked if he'd like his sister and me to make dinner for him on his birthday. Because he's in the midst of moving, he asked if we could delay it for a couple of days.

Sure, I told him. We just didn't want your birthday to go unobserved.

"Well," he said, "There's nothing special about 24."

When his sister turned 21, I wrote about that important milestone in an op-ed piece. I reminisced about her childhood and commented on how proud I was of the young woman she had become.

When Chris turned 21, I knew I couldn't do the same piece twice. I wasn't writing a column yet, so I didn't have a forum to wish him a happy 21st.

He's never let me live that down.

CHRISTOPHER

So, Christopher, on this non-milestone of a birthday, it's your turn.

You decided to make your entry into the world two weeks early. Patience never was your strong suit. It was the first time you asserted yourself. It certainly wasn't the last. From the hour of your birth, you announced you were going to do things your way.

Labor and delivery were hard. The first time I held you close and fed you, you threw up on me.

From the time you could crawl, you never took the easy route. You didn't just prefer to walk to the beat of a different drummer - you wanted to write your own music.

There were times when I wanted to tear my hair out. When you rebelled, when you missed curfew, when your grades sank like a stone, I lay awake nights wondering what I was doing wrong.

You always took things hard. A harsh word from someone you cared about could wound you deeply. A lecture could destroy you for days, no matter how much I tried to inject a positive note about what you'd done right with each admonition about what you'd done wrong.

And you did so many things right.

You've always been generous. If someone needs it, you gladly give it away. I can't count the number of compliments I've had about how polite you are.

Even as an adolescent, you were loyal to a fault. You never picked your friends based on what others said about them. You became the one they turned to when they needed advice.

You have an uncommon sweetness and a wicked sense of humor. As your Aunt Billie says, "Chris can always make me laugh."

You have a poet's soul.

You have a gentle and tender heart. Once, when you were 3 and your sister pushed you too far and you'd had enough, you socked her. The minute she began to cry, your scowl softened and you, too, dissolved in tears, putting your arms around her to comfort her. You never could stand to see anyone hurt.

You've always been there for her, as she has been for you. Do you remember how, as a toddler, you would crawl to her room at night and sleep on the floor beside her bed, just to be near her?

You forgive easily. No matter how mad you are at someone, you never withhold your love.

You complain that I expect too much from you. Know this: all I want is for you to be happy and productive, making an honest living at something you like. To always strive to do the right thing, the decent thing and to be dependable, a man of your word.

I'm proud of the man you've become. You've had some bitter disappointments and difficult circumstances. I respect you for facing them head on, rather than running away.

You set goals for yourself - never designed to impress others - and you met them. I'm proud of your individuality.

You often made things more difficult than they had to be. But if I have learned one thing about raising children, it is this: the harder the journey, the sweeter the arrival.

Once, when I asked you if - even during the times I was hardest on you - you understood that I would always be there for you, you said, "Mom, I have never felt unloved, even for a minute."

It was more than I could have hoped for. The one message I was determined to give to you - the security of unconditional love - got through.

Which brings us back to that phone call.

"What do you want for your birthday?" I asked.

"Just your love," you answered.

It's the easiest gift I've ever given.

Family's gift keeps child's memory alive
July 14, 1995

I met Sunny when she was 3. She was as vibrant and alive as any child I've known - even as cancer was stretching dark fingers through her little body.

Sunny spent a lot of time at Texas Children's Hospital in Houston. I went there to do a story about the hospital's annual art exhibit that featured works by children with cancer.

Sunny greeted me with a radiant smile and ferocious hug. I held her in my arms as we walked around the lobby and looked at the colorful drawings, essays and poetry that told the stories of how it felt to have cancer.

Sunny's painting was titled, "Me and My IV Pole." It showed her standing beneath a rainbow, her constant companion of metal and tubing at her side.

At the end of the morning, Sunny took me by the hand and led me to a couch, stood on it and pulled my arms around her. She then insisted that her Mom take our picture.

That was in October, 1993.

This past week, Sunny's dad came to see me, carrying a plastic bag in his hands.

"Do you remember me?" he asked.

The question stunned me. How could I not? I had been instantly drawn to him and his family, and grew to respect their courage, dignity and faith. A year ago, I sat in the church at Sunny's memorial service and watched her family tell her goodbye. I listened to the beautiful remembrances of her abbreviated life by those who loved her well.

I took her dad to an empty office so we could have a moment of privacy.

"We wanted you to have this," he said, reaching into the bag to pull out "Me and My IV Pole." He turned it over and showed me the back. Sunny's siblings had carefully cut out the story I had done on her and the art exhibit, added a hand-written note of thanks and glued them to the back. He paused a moment for composure.

"We wanted to give it to you before, but . . ."

It was my turn to fight for composure.

"No, please. You should keep this," I urged.

"We want you to have it. We just couldn't part with it yet," he continued, his face wet with tears. "But this is why we now can."

He reached into the plastic bag and pulled out another piece of art, the last Sunny created. There is a rainbow in it as well, but this one has vivid colors, a marked contrast to the one I now held in my hands, a somber study in brown and yellow.

There was another remarkable difference.

This time, the IV pole was gone, and Sunny wasn't anchored to the ground, but soaring high above the rainbow.

"I think, somehow, she knew," her dad said.

When I first wrote about this incredible little girl, I did the story the way I was supposed to. I talked about her family and struggle with cancer. I quoted the therapists at the hospital who use art to help the children work through their feelings. I told about the exhibit and described some of the paintings. The facts were there.

But the essence of who this child was and what she meant to her family was not.

There are stories you cover that make you sad. And there are stories that tear your heart in two, no matter how hard you try not to let them.

And once in while, a very great while, there is a story that touches you so profoundly your life is forever changed. That is what Sunny did for me.

Trying to express what being included in this family's life has meant to me is an effort in futility. It doesn't speak to the everyday, ordinary movements we go through in the process of living.

It speaks to the spirit, and to the heart. Places where few people outside ourselves can go, or understand, even when we try to let them in.

It's easy to understand how Sunny came by her remarkable spirit. It is the same one alive and well in her mother, her father and her brothers and sisters, who carry on with those ordinary movements, even when their heart-sick souls tell them they surely cannot.

It's also easy to spot those special souls, hand-picked by God to be His messengers on earth. Sunny was one.

And so are the mother and father who can gift a writer – someone who did nothing more than share the story of a few fleeting hours with their child - with one of their most precious remembrances.

"We hope it will be a blessing to you," her dad said.

If only he knew how much.

Hubby digs lean, green mowing machine
July 28, 1995

What is it about men and machines?

If you ask a group of men to describe what their wife was wearing and where they went on their first date, most of them would be clueless. Ask that same group of men what model their first car was and they'll tell you what year, what make, how big the engine was, how many barrels the carburetor had, whether it had dual exhausts, how many gallons the gas tank held and how many miles to the gallon it got.

They'll lovingly describe the tires, the hubcaps, the upholstery, the gearshift knob. They will wax nostalgic about how many seconds it would take to reach 60 mph and where the speedometer would max out.

They'll tell you how much it cost, how much their notes were and how much they insured it for. They'll describe the color in decorator-detail.

Their mechanical fascination doesn't stop with cars.

Case in point.

Every week or so, Hubby takes a stroll out back, looks at the knee-deep grass and says, "Well, I guess I have to wait another couple of days before I can mow. It's just too wet. You know, all that rain we've had."

Days later, he looks skyward and pronounces, "Looks like it's gonna break loose at any time. See those dark clouds? Maybe tomorrow."

By the weekend, "It's too hot to mow. I'll wait until it cools off."

Get the picture?

All that has changed. Hubby has a new machine.

It's a bright, shiny, lean green, mowing machine.

You should have seen him at the dealership when he was picking it out. He walked from model to model, checking out the horsepower, the transmission and the width of the cut. He asked about air-cooled engines and water-cooled and whether it had attachments.

He ran his hands lovingly over the hood, caressing the machine's sleek curves. I was beginning to feel jealous.

When he had it delivered, the salesman unloaded the mower, then spent a few minutes explaining how everything worked. I could see my husband's fingers twitching. He was so impatient to turn the ignition key and sit in the driver's seat he could barely feign any interest in the instructions. This really worried me because I knew the instruction manual was more likely to be made into a feature film than be read by the Male Operator.

Hubby was trembling so much in anticipation I had visions of him shoving the salesman out of the way and running him over.

Sure enough, as soon as the salesman stopped talking and stepped back, Hubby was off and running. Or, I should say, holding on for dear life.

Seems Hubby, accustomed to our old lawnmower, was unaware how much more power this lean, green mowing machine had. It took off like a bucking bronco, briefly flinging him backward before snapping him upright again, like some landscape cowboy.

He missed the salesman's open truck door – and the fence on the other side – by inches.

The salesman grinned, having had much experience with other New Male Operators, I should think.

It was about this time that our friend Gene arrived to pick us up for a social engagement. He looked at The Machine, looked at Hubby and said to the salesman, "Do you have a card? I've been thinking about getting a new mower."

"What size are you interested in?" the salesman asked.

Our friend pointed to The Machine and said in a lustful tone, "Just like that one."

Now, every few days, Hubby strolls out back, leaps adventurously onto The Machine, fires it up and is off and racing. He mows, then re-mows. When it's mulched so much there's nothing left to run over, he just raises the mower and speeds around the lawn doing figure eights.

I no longer worry about the grass getting knee deep. Instead, I worry about it dying from being over mowed.

And I worry that, as more Males come to take a peek at The Machine, Hubby will start getting more calls from their wives.

Like the one from Myra, our friend's wife.

"Guess what's in my backyard?" she asked Hubby through clenched teeth.

"I don't know," he said. "What?"

"Well," she said. "I'll give you a hint. It's green."

Passing the recipe torch
Feb 9, 1996

I was thumbing through cookbooks recently, looking for a good recipe for a breakfast casserole. We were invited to friends' and knew it would be a late evening. Our hosts had decided we should bring something different in the food department.

I did find a recipe or two I liked, but I wanted to have at least one more choice because of the size of the gathering. Since I planned to take two dishes, I was hoping to find a particular recipe for a breakfast pizza.

None of my books had it, so I decided to call my daughter and have her check her cookbooks.

When she answered the phone, we chatted for a minute, then I told her what I wanted. Could you look in your cookbooks and see if you can find one? I asked.

"Mom!"

"What?" I said in response to her exclamatory tone.

"I can't believe this," she said.

"Believe what?"

"That YOU called ME to ask for a recipe."

"Do you realize," she continued," that this is the first time you've ever asked me for a recipe?"

You couldn't miss the pleasure in her voice. It made me smile, imagining her smile on the other end of the line.

I hadn't given it a second thought when I called her. Suddenly, I found myself thinking about those rites of passage that we traverse as daughters and mothers.

When my daughter first was married, she took a lot of teasing from her new husband about her lack of cooking skills. To be fair, she did know the basics already, having lived on her own in an apartment for some time and having managed quite nicely.

The first time she cooked for us, she searched our faces as we ate and noted whether we asked for seconds. Even now, she is pleased to discover that we really like what she cooks.

Stephanie has turned into a very good cook, mastering dishes that aren't in my repertoire. Because her husband is an avid outdoorsman, she cooks things I would shudder to see and never would deign to touch. Things I feel compelled to administer last rites to – and I'm not even Catholic.

Not long ago, when I bought a buttermilk pie from a restaurant in Columbus – the best I've ever had – she agreed that it was wonderful.

Later, she found several recipes and called me to compare them to the restaurant's recipe, which they had given me but which makes 10 pies at one time. I relayed to her the restaurant chef's hint that browning the butter gives the pie its distinct flavor.

She called back the next night and said, "Mom, you won't believe how good this pie is. It is just as good as the one in the restaurant. It is SOOOOOOOO good."

It was so good, she continued, that her husband praised it – as did her mother-in-law, who is a fabulous cook.

This didn't surprise me at all. It's been a long time since I've thought her a fledgling girl-child. In my eyes, she's been a woman in her own right for quite some time.

Still, to her, it must seem as if I will always view her exclusively as the child. I can't imagine why. I mean, don't all mothers ask their children to call them when they get home so they'll know they made it safely? Don't all mothers relate horror stories as a way of continuing to remind them to lock their car doors?

I can feel the next, inevitable rite-of-passage coming.

It won't be long until she is bringing dishes to family dinners –

dishes that she has become famous for. And it won't be long after until she will make the turkey for Thanksgiving and we'll gather at her home.

Through the years, my daughter and I have shared many phone conversations. We talk often, discussions that ebb and flow with our lives. I would be lying if I didn't admit that those conversations make me ridiculously happy. I feel lucky she wants to talk with me about her life.

If my luck continues, no matter how good a cook she becomes, or how successful in living life with complete confidence she grows, once in a while, she will still need me.

If only for a recipe.

Trio of terrorists
Dec. 20 1996

I've been accused of many things in my life, but no one ever has mistaken me for a terrorist - until this past weekend.

My brother, David, and I were scheduled to fly home together after a trip to Arkansas. He would deplane in Dallas and I would continue to Houston.

We arrived at the airport in Little Rock an hour before our flight. Dave likes to be early so he can find an empty luggage bin for the case that holds his cherished Martin guitar.

When we arrived, I went to the counter and paid for my ticket while Dave and my other brother, Carl, went to park and to bring in our luggage.

I went through security and waited for my brothers to catch up. I sat down while they went to the gate counter to get our boarding passes. After a few minutes they came back and said, "You're not going to believe this, but we have to take our luggage and go back through security again."

"Why?" I asked.

"That's what we asked," Dave said, "but she wouldn't tell us. She just shoved this piece of paper across the counter that said she couldn't discuss it."

At first, I thought they were kidding. It's just the kind of joke they're always playing on each other. In the past, they've put smoke bombs under car hoods and taped metal washers to the top of bedroom ceiling fans just to torture each other with the sound of unbalanced blades going "whomp, whomp, whomp" all night.

No, they assured me. They were not kidding.

Obviously, I said, we fit some kind of profile; but why?

I looked at Carl, an ordinary-looking guy, dressed reasonably neatly in a T-shirt and shorts. I looked down at myself. I had on leggings and a matching tunic and carried a sedate leather wallet purse and bag.

Carl and I turned and looked at Dave. "Hey," he said a tad

CARL AND DAVID

defensibly, "a man's got a right to travel comfortably."

Dave hadn't shaved in a couple of days. He was wearing his favorite, well-worn black jeans, a rumpled plaid shirt, black suspenders and tennis shoes that looked like they'd spent a few years in places you wouldn't want to know about. I particularly liked the baseball cap that said, "Carl's Corner, Texas."

Granted, he might not have stepped out of the pages of GQ - he'd die before he'd stoop so low as to look like a yuppie - but he didn't look threatening.

"Hey," Dave said to Carl. "If they're looking for suspicious types, why didn't they go after this guy?"

We looked across the waiting room at a man who looked like the lead actor in every bad commando movie made. He wore a black beret, camouflage pants with eight or ten pockets – all bulging – a leather flak jacket with stuffed pockets of its own, and a leather holster-type belt.

And they didn't detain him. Why us?

The boys hauled the luggage back through security, where guards thoroughly searched it. Did they look inside the guitar case? The big, roomy case that could have held just about anything? Nope. And, of course, Dave felt it necessary to torture me with a description of my underwear draped across the security guard's arm. "I think he liked it a little too much," he said.

A few minutes after the Great Luggage Molestation, we looked up to see the two security guards headed to our section of the waiting room. They took spots across from us and leaned against the wall.

"Something's going down, Man," my brother said in his best Cheech Marin voice.

"Please behave," I begged, picturing us behind bars. "This could be serious and I'd like to get home tonight."

"Well, the way I figure it," Carl said, "They'll let everyone else get on the plane, then politely say, 'Come with us please.' "

"Surely not," I said. "Look at us. Why would anyone think we were about to sabotage a plane?"

I'm still wondering. A few minutes before time to board, the security guards took one more look around and left.

Us? Dangerous? It's a concept that still makes me laugh.

My brothers are a threat - but only to each other.

Grandmother's lessons last a lifetime
Feb 21, 1997

The closer we got to Bea's home, the more I wondered how my husband would handle seeing her.

He'd had a year to adjust to the changes in his grandmother. At her 90th birthday party, he had noted the frailty of her tiny frame and had seen cloudiness veil the blue eyes so like his own.

We had heard his parents talk about her continuing descent into a place no one else could go. There are days when she seems like herself and days when she doesn't recognize anyone.

Bea has been lucky. She has lived a full life. Her health has been remarkably good, but the sharpness of her mind has been an even richer blessing.

My husband knows that is no longer the case, but there is a painful chasm between knowing and accepting.

It was Bea who made certain he got his first bike the Christmas there wasn't enough money to go round.

"If he wants a bike, he's going to have one," Granny Bea said.

You didn't argue with Bea. She might have been tiny, but she was mighty. Her tongue was as sharp as her heart was tender. It only took one time being on the receiving end to know you didn't want to go there again.

The only person who wasn't wary of her temper was her husband, George, a good natured man with the kind of patience others envy. He would intentionally get her dander up and then laugh merrily as she gave him what for.

He'd stand behind her and make faces for the grandchildren, who'd laugh with him until she figured out he was mimicking her, then scatter to safety.

Of all the lessons he has learned from his grandmother, my husband says, the most significant is that family is the most important thing in life.

DALE, BEA AND ALTA

Bea practiced what she preached. Big dinners were standard at her home. When the overflow spilled into the garage, she had it carpeted and set out extra tables.

When her mother no longer could care for herself, Bea took her in, just as my in-laws have done for Bea.

When my husband and I fell in love, it was Bea he invited to share his happiness. She was the first to learn the baby of the family was getting married.

If anyone could understand him marrying a woman with two children, he said, it was Bea. She had three children when George married her, and he loved them unconditionally.

Bea knew what my husband faced from family members who would rather he marry a woman who would give him his "own" children. If she had any reservations, Bea never showed them. She was happy for him and gave him the blessing he so wanted.

My father-in-law, who has been so good to Bea and sometimes is the only one to whom she will listen when she becomes agitated, says keeping a sense of humor is the best way he knows to handle this difficult situation.

It is he who disconnected the gas to the stove and fetched her when she wandered off in the middle of the night. It is he who dressed her when he found her sitting on the couch naked, complaining, "Dale, it's cold in here. Why won't you turn the heat on?"

My father-in-law relates stories of watching Bea stand in front of the mirrored closet in her bedroom and argue with the young woman she is convinced lives there.

"Now you listen to me young lady," she admonished as she shook a finger at her image, "You can just go to hell, because we're just trying to help you, you know."

As my husband spent time with Bea earlier this month, his inability to close the mental distance between them was a hurt like no other for the grandson who always felt her favorite.

When it was time to say goodbye, I leaned over and gave Bea a kiss,

---

Bea's family, back, from left: Alta Melvin McBride (Joel's mom), Jimmy Taylor, and Virginia Taylor, front: George Taylor, G.R. Taylor and Bea Butterfield Taylor

then watched as he did the same.

"I love you," she said to him, and I watched her eyes scan his face, and his, hers.

"I love you, too," he told her, then kissed her and quickly walked away.

We didn't talk about it on the eight-hour drive home. We know what lies in store, and what a loss it will be, but the chasm between knowing and accepting never loomed larger.

When I encounter disappointment and lose my perspective about life, it is most often my husband who pulls me back and reminds me what matters most.

I shouldn't be surprised.

He had a good teacher.

Father's Day
June 15, 1997

I spent the first half of my life looking for my father. I will spend the second half missing him. In between, I had five years and three months.

My mother and father had a World War II-era love affair and I was the product. Although they loved each other, societal pressures and the disapproval of my father's strict religious family drove my mother to return to a loveless marriage.

I grew up knowing there was some secret concerning me. It shaped my life in ways both subtle and profound. I heard the first hint of the truth at 15. Years later, when I confronted my mother and the man I believed was my father, they both denied it.

My mother and her husband divorced when I was 3 months old. My grandparents raised me in a good home, but everything was colored with the absence of a father and mother.

I tortured myself wondering why they didn't want me and grew up thinking I must be unlovable.

In 1991, my mother chose to tell me the truth. We met for lunch and she shoved a photo across the table.

"Is that my father?" I asked, my heart caught in my throat and breathing suddenly an impossibility.

"Yes," she said, "and you need to know that he didn't leave us. I left him. I didn't tell him I was pregnant. He didn't learn about you until after you were born. He didn't want me to go back to my marriage, but I told him it was my decision and if he loved me at all, he would respect it."

I called my father that night, unsure of what I would say. Of what he would say. What kind of a man was he? Would he find me unlovable as well?

"Hi. This is Jane. I understand you're my father."

"Well hello, Love," he said. "Yes I am, and there hasn't been one day since I learned about you that I haven't thought about you."

I wept through the entire conversation. I could hear his own tears.

I went to Arkansas to meet him. I learned how like him I am, not only in looks, but in philosophy and personality. For the first time in my life, I felt complete.

I visited often and talked to my dad at least ever other weekend. We never spoke that he didn't tell me he loved me. The first time he sent me a card I was overwhelmed by the signature, "Love, Dad."

That first Father's Day, I sent him three cards. One wouldn't do. When I became a columnist, I delayed the first column until the week of Father's Day so it could be about him.

I began to understand why I'd always felt different. I found my heritage and my genes. And even through the emotion, I could understand why I had the best of everything.

My father never once said anything critical about me. We never had a cross word. There was no baggage from childhood to overcome. There was only love. The radiant, accepting kind of love you feel when you finally find what was stolen from you.

Each time we talked, I chided Dad about taking care of his health.

"It took me too many years to find you," I told him. "Don't let me lose you now."

My father died unexpectedly in his sleep just before Christmas.

It is impossible to describe the loss I feel. I never knew you could hurt so much and still go about the business of breathing.

I was honored to deliver his eulogy. I told a roomful of people, most of whom had never met me and many of whom didn't know I existed, what he meant to me and the kind of man I found him to be. I spoke of the years I had lost and how much I had gained. How much I could have missed had I not been given the gift of my father.

As I leaned over the casket to tell him I loved him and to say goodbye, I whispered a promise that I would never forget him.

Each Sunday, I still want to reach for the phone. The feeling is so intense that one day, I just gave in. Of course there was no answer, but it helped me to feel connected in some small way, even as it helped me begin to accept that he was gone.

For a while, I lost the desire to complete my genealogy chart. I would open dad's page and look at the line that said, date of death. I couldn't fill it in.

Six months later, I'm still struggling with letting him go.

I had my father five years and three months.

It wasn't long enough.

Happy Father's Day, Dad.

Little Rock desegregation close to home
Sept. 21, 1997

In 1957, when I was an adolescent living in Arkansas, the confusing images of Little Rock's Central High School forced desegregation were a disturbing introduction to bigotry and hatred.

I was too young to intellectualize what I saw. I could only react to the tightening in my stomach when I saw the photographs of a young black girl walking through a fearsome and hate-filled crowd of whites.

For days, I listened to loud and insistent voices cheering Gov. Orval Faubus' efforts to postpone what many refused to admit was inevitable – and right.

The voices I heard that questioned the morality of segregation were tentative and few – and most came from "outsiders."

The tension in my world escalated right along with the desegregation of the school a couple of hours from where I lived. When my grandfather yelled at the television commentators and, cursing, left the room, the tightening worsened.

Prejudice was my heritage – a way of thinking that had been passed from parent to child, just as it had been in other regions of the country.

I have no way of knowing what influences or events caused the people around me to slip further into the abyss of bigotry. I know ignorance and isolation played the greatest part.

But I clearly remember the unsettling feeling that things would never again be the same for our family.

It was, for me, the moment when I first understood that even the most loving and generous of us could harbor an equal amount of ignorance and intolerance.

I remember Moses, a black man who helped my grandfather butcher hogs. One fall day, my grandmother, grandfather and I sat down and ate.

When we finished my grandmother fixed a plate for Moses. Instead of taking it outside to him, she called him to the table.

I saw the look my grandmother and grandfather exchanged. His was one of anger. Hers was defiance.

It is hard for young people today, not of my rural upbringing and not of my generation, to understand this scene. My grandmother's rebellion stood out in the days when blacks did not sit down with whites.

My grandmother died when I was 20, so I cannot ask what compelled her to defy my grandfather. Knowing her heart, I suspect I know.

Moses also knew my grandmother's heart. He was one of several blacks to pay their respects at her funeral.

The confusion I felt while watching our state's schools become desegregated, and my feelings of disloyalty to my family, stayed with me for years. As I learned more about the world around me and was exposed to other ways of thinking, I became more certain of what I believed.

Later, as a high school student, I would incur my grandfather's wrath when I dared speak out at the dinner table in favor of civil rights. Incensed, he threw a butter knife across the table, hitting me just below the eye.

Bigotry knows no color. It comes in all peoples and wears many faces. The most obvious are racial and cultural, but there also are intellectual bigots who think a lack of education indicates inferiority and religious bigots who dismiss some of the most decent and pious among us simply because their religion follows another path to righteousness.

There are bigots in the work force who equate a title with superiority. There are class bigots who think a paycheck denotes sovereignty.

The battle against prejudices that live within us all is a life-long one. Mine began with the image of a frightened but determined young girl, who, other than the color of her skin, could have been me.

These days, when we hear the phrase "the power of the media," it often is used as an epithet, hurled at those who deliver the news.

It was the media that brought me the images that changed my life. It was the media that made me think. Made me question. Made me wonder what else I didn't know.

Those images, forever etched in my memory, were burned into my consciousness by journalists whose work I respect.

And in whose debt I remain.

There is power in the media. And when we do it right, we can change the world. Not by promoting an agenda, but by reflecting words and images of the world around us.

We give those words and images to you. What you do with them is your choice.

Section Three

October 17, 1997 to April 22, 2001

STEPHANIE AND HER SONS, JORDAN, ON LEFT,
AND JARROD, ON RIGHT.

Grandson's birth completes love's cycle

Oct. 17, 1997

Becoming a grandmother wasn't what I expected.

I've heard friends speak about the joy they feel when they first see their grandchildren. I have listened to them falter as they try to describe that love.

That is exactly what I expected to describe in this column. What I didn't expect was where my focus would be - or its intensity.

My daughter is an independent young woman. She left the cuddly stage behind as a child, allowing only quick hugs widely spaced. Although she has a heart capable of abundant love, she expresses it more comfortably in words than in physical displays.

I've missed those lingering hugs and soft kisses.

Some children turn to a parent for comfort during stress or hurt. Others pull into themselves while they fight to get back the control that is so important to them. My eldest is the latter.

I was fortunate to be with her when she went for her regular obstetrical visit and discovered she was in labor. Her pregnancy had been uneventful and the contractions so mild she wasn't aware she was having them. When the doctor told her he wanted her to go to the hospital – yes, right now, please – she was speechless.

She turned to me with wide eyes and for just a moment, she was a child again. A child who needed her mommy.

She called her husband (who had just gotten home from work) to tell him the news. We walked next door to the hospital and checked in to begin the baby wait.

When the contractions intensified and the doctor came in, we all stepped outside. My son-in-law came out and told us she was having a difficult time relaxing between contractions and they thought maybe it would be best if they were alone the rest of the way.

We all understood and told him so.

An hour or two later, he stepped outside, looked at me and said, "Mom. She's asking for you."

I feel so blessed to have shared the next few hours with them. I watched the fierce determination with which my daughter worked to bring her much-anticipated baby into the world.

When it came time for her to deliver, I stepped outside so they could share that time alone, as a couple, before they became three.

After the baby was born, after everyone gave their congratulations and marveled at the baby and said good-bye, my son-in-law turned to me and said, "You know, I've heard my friends say how worried they were that something would be wrong with their baby. It never occurred to me to worry about that."

I suddenly realized that it had been the same for me, but for a different reason. All my energies, all my thoughts, all my love had been focused on my child. It was her I worried about. Her pain I longed to ease.

Later, I went home, crawled into my husband's waiting arms and fell asleep, knowing how blessed we are.

Welcome, little Jordan Zane. You fill our hearts. Your Poppie and I already are smitten and we pledge to always be there for you.

And we hope you give your mommy a lifetime of lingering hugs and soft kisses.

Welcome to the world, Jarrod
Feb. 7, 1999

A year and four months ago, I held our grandson close, eager to establish a connection to the child whose birth had been so eagerly awaited. This past week, I got to do it again.

It was 4:30 a.m. when the phone rang. "It's the baby," I said, waking my husband.

In one of those moments of serendipity that no longer surprise me, I already was awake - had been for at least half an hour. I had fallen asleep early the night before, exhausted from unsuccessfully fighting a nasty head cold.

So I did what I often do in those quiet moments when all you hear is the sound of your own thoughts: I gave thanks for the blessings of the day and began praying for those in my life facing difficulties - and for the health of my daughter and her unborn child.

I didn't know that as I prayed, she and her husband were already at the hospital, preparing to welcome their new son.

As I dressed to go to them, I reviewed the past couple of days: yes, my head was stopped up and my stomach had been queasy, but there had been no fever. Was it a virus? Was I contagious?

I never considered not going to the hospital. Only God could have kept me from at least being near my daughter during labor and delivery. But I did think about putting the baby at risk.

So I stood by as everyone, one by one, welcomed him. It would be late that day before I allowed myself to touch him, a tentative stroke of fingertip against that wonderful, silken baby skin.

I consoled myself those first hours and days with the knowledge that touch can take other forms. I held this baby in my heart.

I heard him cry before I saw him, a plaintive, hurt whimper that pierced my soul. His big brother's first cry had been assertive, a strong, I'm-not-happy cry. This was a pleading, hold-me-I-need-you cry that made me want to scoop him up, croon to him and cover his face with kisses.

We are taking great pains, his Poppie and I, not to compare these babies too much. We are grateful to have two boys to love, and we celebrate their individuality.

This child, inevitably, will face comparison to his big brother, especially since they are so close in age. Jordan has been much beloved, his every move chronicled by we who take such delight in him.

And yes, Jarrod does look somewhat like Jordan did when he was born. But he is very much his own person, with beautiful long, expressive hands and finely-sculpted features.

So we make this promise to you, Jarrod. We will rejoice in all those special, one-of-a-kind things that make you, you. We will love you with a love unlike that we have for anyone else. It will be Jarrod love, freely given.

We will seek out special time to spend just with you. To watch as you grow into the person only you can become.

Your mom tells me she can hardly bear to put you down to sleep. All week, she has held you close, marveling at your sweetness. You are a good baby, a placid baby who almost never cries; when you do, she sings you a special lullaby, with words chosen only for you.

Tonight, I will go to you, scoop you in my arms, croon to you and cover your face with kisses.

And later, as I lie in the darkness preparing to sleep, I will give thanks for the blessings of this day, and for a wee babe who holds my heart in his tiny hands.

Father's love will outlast loss

June 20, 1999

It begins the third week or so each June with a heaviness that settles in and refuses to leave. A tenacious melancholy cloaks every waking moment and clings stubbornly to the subconscious, even in sleep.

Awakening, heavy of lid and heart, I long to close my eyes, press my face into the comforting softness of the pillow and return to the undemanding state somewhere between waking and sleep that guards against concrete thought. Sleep holds more promise than consciousness.

A vague sense that something isn't right gives way to full-blown misery. I don't want to talk. I don't want to socialize. Prone to relentless introspection, I suddenly don't want to think.

And I can't say why.

It's been that way for three years. You'd think by now I'd know at the first twinge of unease what is happening. But I don't.

Because I don't want to remember that my father is dead.

Father's Day and I have a long history of animosity. As a child being raised by grandparents, it was a bitter reminder that I was of so little regard to my father that I'd never seen his face or heard him speak.

As a teen-ager, it was a hateful recollection that the name on the line that said "Father" on my birth certificate was a lie. I couldn't prove it – but I knew it to be so.

As a young mother, it was a cruel reminder that I was powerless to know my father unless the one person who knew the truth would share it.

I would be in my 40s before that would happen and I would finally meet Dad.

For five years, Father's Day became a joyful celebration. I had a father who loved me, who thought I was smart and funny and who cherished every minute I spent with him. Who was comforted by the joy I took in my two newly discovered brothers, whom I loved almost on sight.

And then he died.

Once again, Father's Day was filled with an overpowering sense of loss.

It is not my nature to dwell on what I don't have. I am usually appreciative of the many blessings a generous God bestows. I can delight in small treasures and great gifts.

But I am not yet able to let the gratefulness I feel for the five years and three months I had with my father carry more weight on this day than the sadness I feel at his absence.

I believe that day will come. When I remember that I no longer have to wonder what it would be like to see the words "Love, Dad" written to me. When I rejoice in finally laying to rest the lifelong sense of being nobody's child.

Earlier this week, when the burden felt unbearable, I drove to my husband's workplace, closed the door to his office and lost myself in his arms.

It was a potent, tangible reminder of the power of love to hold at bay what hurts us most.

That's what my dad did, just by loving me.

It's what I want to do - what I hope to do - for my children.

So, to cope, I sleep later than usual, take all the hugs I can get and, when I feel I need it most, close my eyes and remember the sound of my father's voice as he told me he loved me.

For now, it is enough.

A generous heart
April 16, 2000

My daughter is a joyful breath of fresh air with a sunny disposition and a compassionate heart. People naturally are drawn to her.

Because she changed jobs about a year ago, she's recently made some new friends. One of them, with whom she felt an immediate affinity, invited Steph to a girl's weekend in Philadelphia.

She looked forward to it for months.

It wasn't easy to arrange. She has two toddlers 16 months apart and a husband whose job frequently requires weekend work and overtime.

She has a demanding career that challenges her daily, which she loves. God certainly directed her to her chosen profession (human resource management) because she is a natural-born mediator. She is logical and levelheaded, with a genuine concern for others. She loves finding the most equitable solution to a problem.

She called me the day after she got home. "Just tell me it was wonderful," I said, needing to hear that the three days she had away from the demands of work, wifedom and motherhood had been restful and refreshing, which is just what my mother's heart wanted for her. I worry that she doesn't get much of either – and probably won't until the boys get older.

Yes, she said, she did have a great time, although she really missed being away from her babies and husband.

When women get together, they share their feelings on most everything, especially relationships. Their conversation eventually turned to mothers and daughters, which won't surprise any female reading this.

I held my breath.

"You know," Steph said (and I paraphrase here), "a couple of them talked at length about the troubled relationships they have with their mothers. One has grown weary with her mother's fault-finding and has given up any hope of having a relationship with her.

"As I listened to them," she added, "I felt so sad. They're still carrying those wounds around. It influences how they view themselves and how they interact with others. I know you understand that," she said.

I do.

And then, this beautiful child of mine said, "I told my friend that the first thing I was going to do when I got home was hug my mother."

"Yes, you really get on my nerves sometimes," she said (like this was any big surprise), "and I know I drive you crazy" (absolutely not true) "but I know that you love and support me and you always want only the best for me."

And what I know, I thought as I hung up the phone, is the other half of this equation - the thing that makes it work.

I have a daughter who embraces the good in life. She never dwells on past mistakes, and is generous, truly, to a fault. Her forgiving heart is quick to overlook shortcomings and celebrate the best in us.

That's why she makes a great manager – and the world's best daughter.

Stephanie, forget about that holiday coming up in a few weeks. I don't need a Mother's Day present.

I already have you.

Beatle Love
Sunday, December 10, 2000

It is late in the afternoon. The temperature in the upstairs bedroom of the aging two-story white house on Maple Street has peaked, and a timid breeze promises relief.

The constant low hum of the refinery next door seeps through the cracks in the casement. It, along with the intermittent sound of sibling squabbles, is the soundtrack of our lives.

My sister, being a good Southern girl, carries two names that are uttered as one. "BillieJean," I can hear the call floating up the stairs, in the voice of one of my brothers or sisters.

"Billie Jean, telephone." The call is repeated several times a day.

Sometimes it's "Anita Sue, telephone." Charles William and John Wesley and Judy Gail and Susan Marie are too young yet to get many calls.

The days change. The sounds do not.

Until the summer of 1964, when Billie Jean falls in love, deeply, passionately, for perhaps the first time.

The soundtrack of her life has changed. She never again will be able to think of this year without hearing the voice.

The one that sings, "She loves, you, yeah, yeah, yeah, she loves you, yeah, yeah, yeah, yeah."

Billie has found the Beatles, and Paul has become her touchstone, just as John has become Anita's. They immerse themselves in studying their idols; ask any question and they can answer it.

"How tall is John?" "What color eyes does Ringo have?" "Who is the oldest? The youngest?" "What was the name of the club where they first played?"

Our mothers had Frank Sinatra. We had the Beatles. Our children had George Michael and Duran Duran and girls today have 'N Sync and the Backstreet Boys.

We smile and speak offhandedly about the infatuations we had in common. "Gosh, weren't we silly?" we joke.

But beneath the casual dismissal, the 13-year-olds we once were are protesting our disloyalty. We have betrayed the ones we once loved.

Yes, trust me, for some of us, it was that intense.

By the time the boys from Liverpool had come along, I was 15, and beyond their reach.

I already had been in love, with a real person, not an untouchable figure in a fan magazine. I had experienced the sting of rejection and was drawn to mournful tunes like Gene Pitney's "Town Without Pity," Freddy Scott's "Hey, Girl," or Brenda Lee's "Fool Number One."

But I watched my sisters and I read their letters and I saw what the Beatles meant to them.

I can't know what they felt. Only they could say. But I could sleep in a shared bedroom and listen to the record player and absorb a little simply by osmosis.

I wouldn't trade those days and nights for anything.

John Lennon died 20 years ago this past Friday.

His influence lives on, not only in the body of work he produced, but as a permanent imprint on the lives of girls named Billie Jean and Anita Sue who came of age listening to his music.

She loves you yeah, yeah, yeah, yeah.

Twenty years – and counting
December 17, 2000

This past week marked the 20th anniversary of the day my husband and I said, "I do."

Because it fell in the middle of the week, we celebrated early with dinner out and a trip to Houston to finish Christmas shopping.

The night before the anniversary, I was on assignment and didn't get into bed until midnight. The next day, I had pressing deadlines and a heavy workload, so I didn't look up until close to noon, when he called to say, "Happy anniversary," and to invite me to lunch.

I had forgotten it was our anniversary. He knew — and laughed with me. My work schedule wouldn't permit a lunch break. I apologized and told him I'd see him at home later, for a supper of bacon and eggs, which was about all we had in the pantry.

Fifteen years ago, that would have been a tense moment. No matter who had been on the forgetting/busy end, the other would have been hurt and miffed.

My, how 20 years changes things. After two decades of weathering whatever life throws our way, there is an ease we didn't have before. The little things aren't quite as earth-shattering as they once were. Not that forgetting an anniversary is a little thing. It isn't.

But the date is less important than the relationship it marks. We are secure in the commitment, loyalty and love that have grown each day.

We know each other well, though we still manage to spring a surprise now and then. We trust that each other's happiness is uppermost in our minds.

Twenty years with one person teaches you things. Like:

Each of you needs a space that's yours, painted the color you like (whether that's bright pink or deep gray) and has the chair that, in time, has formed perfectly to the shape of you. Your spouse must respect this place and not try to change it.

There is such a thing as too much togetherness. You weren't born one half of a pair. You were born with a personality all your own. Hang on to it.

There is no substitute for trust. A marriage without it is incomplete, and at risk. That doesn't mean trust happens from day one, especially for someone who has been betrayed or deeply hurt. But it should grow every day.

Trust covers much more than fidelity. It's knowing that you come first and your spouse would never do anything to hurt you.

Honesty is critical. Maturity teaches how to share that honesty. It is to build up, not tear down. How can your mate meet your needs if he or she doesn't know what they are?

If you expect your spouse to meet your every need, to agree with all your decisions, and to never be grumpy or selfish, you're living in a dream world. Get over it – and don't take it personally. Get a dog.

Let the little things ride. Forget small slights. If it's really important to him or her, give in.

Don't keep score.

Don't look for hidden meaning. Don't scrutinize each uttered word. If you trust that he or she loves you, you must trust his or her motives.

Don't constantly try to "improve" your spouse. You fell in love with him or her didn't you? Then why do you think all of a sudden you know better who he or she should be and how he or she should think and act? Worry more about your own shortcomings and less about his or hers. You will learn from each other and grow.

My husband knows I'm grumpy in the mornings. He knows there are times I don't want to talk. I just want to be. He lets me have that, even when it's not what he wants.

He loves me. And he knows even bacon and eggs can be a feast when you're eating it with the person who loves you more than anything else in the world.

Commentary on boobs falls flat

February 18, 2001

This past week, I wrote a column about having a mammogram. I joked about how the procedure smushes our tenderest parts. At least two readers didn't find it the least bit funny.

When readers take us to task, we review what we wrote and ask whether we, at the least, could have done a better job, or at the worst, failed our readers in some way.

The first response said, in part, "I hope you do not think the article in Sunday's Profile section was funny. I pray that she hasn't scared first timers. This procedure is to save people's lives. I have had one every year for 20 years and not one time has it hurt. I think Ms. McBride is a crybaby. Shame on you for letting her write such an article." It was signed, "A survivor."

I e-mailed her back, (knowing I am a crybaby), apologizing first, then saying: "My goal was to write a humor column that poked gentle fun at aging and the mammogram process, and tie that to Valentine's Day. I hoped that women who have mammograms would identify with it and be able to have a laugh or two on me. I hoped (they) . . . would be reminded to make that appointment. My intent never was to be indifferent to the plight of women with breast cancer."

I pleaded my case by telling her I had written columns at least twice before about the importance of yearly mammograms. "Even though we try not to write about the same thing twice," I said, "I feel this is important and so I revisit it from time to time . . . I have stressed how women should get a baseline mammogram at age 40. I have encouraged women to get their mammogram each year. I have said that a mammogram is uncomfortable (it is) but it is worth it. It was never my intention to do otherwise."

I mentioned the stories I have written through the years about breast cancer survivors and their battles with this horrible disease. I told her how amazed I have been by those women's resilience, courage and willingness to tell their stories. I even mentioned the recognition I received from the American Cancer Society for that work. (I know, that was shameless, but I felt SO BAD).

Two days later, I received a note in the mail. It said, "Even if a woman should be reminded to get a mammogram, this is still a private and personal thing and not to be written in a column. I love your columns usually, but this was in bad taste."

The second person to take me to task did so in a letter (with no return address). That kind of envelope always makes me nervous, but then I saw the flap was sealed with a heart. How bad can it be, I thought?

It said, "I am a breast cancer survivor. My cancer was caught in the early stages. I am the first one to joke about mammograms, but they really don't hurt. I hope your column will not stop anyone from getting a mammogram because of fear of the pain. If not for a mammogram, I might not be here today." And then this sweet lady wrote, "I'm glad you had yours."

So, to both of you, I offer my thanks for your concern for women everywhere. I promise to recommit myself to carefully considering the words I write.

And I need to stress that a mammogram might be uncomfortable, but it truly is not that bad, even for people like me who have fibrocystic breast disease.

To the writer of the second note, I say, what a dear soul you are to remind me that I could have done a better job of being funny without discouraging someone from having a test she needs.

And thank you for that heart on the back of the envelope. It surely reflects your own caring one.

Two toolboxes per couple

April 22, 2001

One of the major hardware superstores is doing its part for marital bliss — by promoting a pre-filled toolbox for newlyweds.

The store believes every couple needs a toolbox. They choose the most necessary tools and put them in a box, ready to go. They call it the perfect gift for the perfect couple.

Foolish, foolish people.

Anyone who has been married more than a year knows toolboxes don't promote a healthy marriage. They are weapons of war.

Big Mac (that would be my husband, Mr. McBride) likes to tell himself happy little fairy tales in which he's the hero, as in "The Boy Who Always Puts Things Back Where They Belong."

In this never-never land of Big Mac's imagination, the man of the house (only he would say it as THE MAN of the house, growling and beating his chest) has a toolbox with everything he needs. He keeps the box stored where it belongs.

Whenever he finishes a project his wife has whined about for so long he can't ignore it anymore, he puts each tool back in its proper place in the toolbox and puts it away.

Reality bites.

How can a man who can't find his own shoes keep up with tools?

At our house, when I need a tool, it is nowhere to be found. In the toolbox? Get real. In the hardware drawer? Not a chance.

Tools are found only after turning the house upside down. A hammer? On top of the refrigerator, of course. A screwdriver? In the kitchen utensils drawer, silly.

When the frustration became too much to bear, I became the proud owner of my own toolbox.

It changed my life.

I keep my faithful friend in the same place. Always. When I need something, I pull the toolbox out, open it and remove the tool I need. When I'm through, I put it back.

My husband is soooo jealous. He can never find his toolbox (the one JUST like mine). When he does, half the tools are missing.

What does he do? He raids mine.

Why? He knows it will be exactly where it's supposed to be.

So, days later, when I want to hang a picture, I go for the toolbox. It's not there. I go on a search. I find it outside (OUTSIDE!) under the carport. Open. With tools missing.

After a full-grounds search, I locate the missing tools, wipe them down and put them back in the box.

Which I promptly hide in another room.

It only takes one day for the question I know will come.

"Honey, where's your toolbox?" he purrs.

"Where's yours?" I reply.

Silence.

Then the confession. "I haven't seen it in months."

This comes from the man who always tells friends, neighbors and even strangers in line at the grocery store, "She never puts anything back when she's through with it."

He says this because he is seriously delusional. He figures if a tool is out, I must be the culprit. Oh, the fantasies we invent to keep up our self-esteem.

I have a tip for new brides: Buy three tool kits. One for him, one for you and one as a decoy.

Hide your tool kit. Put a big red X on his so he can't say he only used yours because he mistook it for his. Put the third in a closet.

When he loses his, as he will, and asks for yours, which he will, pull out the third and pretend it's yours.

When a tool comes up missing from "your" toolbox (the decoy), he will have to either find his own or buy you a new one.

Meanwhile, your "real" toolbox sits safe and sound in the closet, happily awaiting its rightful owner.

The one with a fairy tale of her own: "The Woman Who Kept A Spotless House."

Section Four

June 17, 2001 to March 30, 2003

JOEL AT 25

Hey, let me tell my side

Sunday, June 17, 2001

By Joel McBride

After nine years of waiting, now I get to tell my side of the story.

Today, on Father Day's, I get to be your guest columnist, and I'd like to make it clear that nothing my wife has ever said about me is true. Well, that's not really true either. I am a smart, funny, kind, good-looking guy. She did say that somewhere, didn't she?

Jane and I have been married for 20 years. Most of you who read her column know about my likes, dislikes and even my faults. Her tales (especially those with gross exaggerations) have provided my friends, co-workers and customers with a steady stream of material.

The day Jane and I got married, I became a father. Stepfather, that is.

Having children when you enter into a marriage is not out of the ordinary these days. The not-so-ordinary thing is I could not have fathered two more wonderful children. Steph and Chris have brought terror, peace, love and a special friendship into my life I would not have wanted to miss.

I have been blessed to be a part of raising these two great kids. As a stepparent, you can't ask for anything better than the chance to be there as they grow up.

Their stepmother, Gwen, and I have a lot in common. We both became parents of children who were not ours. We both nurtured and influenced them the best we could, and with our efforts, plus those of their mother and father, I know we more than succeeded.

In my heart, they will always be my children, too.

Chris lives in Fort Worth, so we have to drive to go visit. When we do, it's nice to see that he hasn't changed from the sweet young boy he was at 10 - back when he made me want to pull my hair out. Don't all children do that, though?

Stephanie lives closer, much to our delight, because she and her husband, Kyle, have provided us with two incredible grandchildren.

Steph was 12 when her mother and I got married - a tough age for a girl. I look at her now, at the woman she has become, and give thanks that she didn't give up on me as a parent.

She's been a wonderful mother to our - or as I like to call them - "my" boys. It's amazing to see the right way to raise children after you have already done your job by trial and error.

Sorry about the errors, guys.

Jordan will be 4 in October and Jarrod will be 3 next January. They have given me, as well as their other grandparents, the most joy, entertainment and love that anyone could ever hope for or imagine having in a lifetime.

Being a stepparent is much like it is to be the original; you lose sleep worrying that they have been in an accident. You worry that they may be the ones who cause an accident. You think about what you tried to teach them and how you tried to raise them, and think, did I do it right?

You never feel really comfortable. At the end of the day, you just have to hope you did everything you could.

I truly am blessed to be a father. Stepfather, that is. Or does it really matter in the end?

To their dad, Jerry, and to all other fathers, especially my own, I hope that this day brings you many wonderful memories.

Cherish each day as if it were the last. You never get them back.

Sometimes stubborn is good

April 29, 2001

At 6 feet, 5 inches, he was impossible to miss.

With blonde hair, blue eyes, a red beard and an infectious grin, he was impossible to ignore.

When I first met the man who has shared my life for 20 years now, I was drawn to his energy and vitality, sense of humor and ease within his own skin.

There was something about this playful, joy-filled man who loved to tease others unmercifully that made me laugh.

I'm still laughing.

The days that I struggled with problems that weighed me down were the days he picked me up and carried me along for the ride. The sheer exuberance with which he attacked life and made the most of it made me believe I could, too.

There are some things that don't exist in his world. They simply aren't allowed. Defeat is one.

He pursued me with a determination and passion that said he would never give up. He made me feel cherished, adored — and, wonder of wonders — worthy.

I was a hard sell, though. I had failed at relationships and marriage already and was reluctant to commit again. I was terrified of making the "wrong" choice for me — and for the one I chose.

I told him all the reasons why I wasn't ready to make any promises: I had been divorced. I was full of insecurity and self-doubt. I was moody, easily wounded and had a tendency to withdraw. I was, at best, a relaxed housekeeper. "No problem," he said. "Sure, you say that now," I told him, "but trust me, you won't like the real me after the glow fades."

I was seriously doubtful of my lovability. I was flawed, and I knew it.

Sooner or later, I was sure, he would, too.

I didn't realize he already knew. What he also knew was something that would take me years to understand. It was OK. We're all flawed. Without exception. That doesn't make us unworthy of love.

I saved the biggest arguments for last. I reminded this man who never had been married that I couldn't have any more children. He knew that, he said, and was willing to make that trade-off.

How do I live with that? I wondered. I cherished my children so much. It was the kind of sacrifice that someone who had a hard time loving herself couldn't easily accept.

"Don't choose me" became my mantra. "You'll regret it."

He says he never has. And because of the love and commitment he has shown to me — and continues to show to my children and our two grandchildren, whom he loves more than seems humanly possible — I believe him.

I know I never have regretted saying yes.

Oh, and there was one more reason, I told him 20 years ago.

I'm older than you. Yes, I look much younger than my age, but that won't always be the case. What happens when it finally catches up with me?

He didn't buy that argument, either. Women live longer than men, he said. That'll make us even.

There is a wonderful quote attributed to "Winnie the Pooh" that speaks to my heart because I understand it so well.

"If you live to be a hundred, I want to live to be a hundred minus one day, so I never have to live without you."

That's the way I feel about the man who wouldn't take no for an answer.

We don't choose the day we will be born. We don't know the day we will die.

Every day in between is a gift.

My husband has given me countless treasures, the most precious of which is his presence.

Happy birthday, Honey. And thanks for choosing me.

Adversity reveals character
September 30, 2001

Life, real life, is not for sissies.

At some point, usually without warning, we will be asked to show what we're made of. We will be asked to make tough decisions. Some of the choices we must make offer little, if any, reward or solace. Often, we understand that the right answer is the one that will be hardest on us.

At some point, we will experience loss. Loss of health or mobility, loss of love or loved ones, loss of income or financial stability, loss of self-confidence, loss of faith in ourselves.

During the past year, I've watched people close to me come face to face with challenges they couldn't have foreseen. Watching them has brought, along with sorrow for what they've had to face, a great respect in how they've chosen to work their way through it.

Whether it's loss of love or an unexpected medical diagnosis, they all, without exception, have shown courage and grace.

The longer we live, the more we understand that none of us will be allowed to merely skim the surface of life. At some point, we will get mired down, sinking long enough to get dirty.

Whether we rise again depends in large part on whether we choose — and it must be a choice — to confront it head on. We must be willing to call on the strength within each of us.

We quickly learn that sharing our struggles with others multiplies that strength.

A friend once discussed his happiness at finally finding the right person to spend the rest of his life with. He'd had failed relationships before and wondered why they hadn't worked out. He described it like this: "I never knew what I was missing, until now."

There's no turning back once that happens. When we are given the precious gift of a partner for life, we commit to being a partner for life, no matter what comes along. Sometimes we are the supporter. Sometimes we must be supported. Both hone us.

One of my friends has experienced more loss than most of us can imagine. She lost her husband, then was diagnosed with a debilitating neurological disease.

Like any of us would, she struggled to understand and accept what lay ahead. She wisely allowed herself the time to mourn the loss of life as she had known it. She then began educating herself about what to expect. She began to plan the rest of her life, with the adjustments she knew she would have to make.

A close family member has a cruel, progressive disease that has robbed her of the ability to work at a career she loves. The search for a diagnosis and treatment has crippled her finances, but not her spirit. When discussing how she handles the constant weakness, frequent pain and the frustration of a body that has betrayed her, she said this:

"There was a Tibetan teacher who liked to tell his students to 'lean into the sharp points.' When life gets hard or confusing, we must lean into the painful, confusing parts. That teacher was last seen during the Chinese invasion of Tibet, walking toward the Chinese troops, rather than away toward India. He really did lean into that sharp point."

She went on to say that it's difficult to lean into something like being unable to support yourself, or to do simple tasks like yard work, or to read, comprehend and retain complex material. But, as she said, "Here it is, and there is no escaping that."

Life is not for sissies. It requires strength and determination. It calls us to draw upon the best parts of ourselves.

And to understand that we needn't do it alone.

Happy Birthday, Jarrod
February 3, 2002

On Wednesday, the most beautiful, loving and intelligent 2-year-old I know turned 3.

Well yes, of course it's my grandchild, but I can assure you everything I've said is true and not just the opinion of a proud Grammie.

Everyone who meets Jarrod is struck by his radiant smile. Even though he's a boy, he's still enough of a baby to be called beautiful.

Until his first haircut this past year (a real heartbreaker for his Grammie and Poppie), Jarrod had blond curls that seemed to grab all the available light in a room into a sunny halo. Few people could resist reaching out to touch them as he walked by. He also has beautiful skin, luminous eyes, an adorable mouth and the briefest hint of dimples.

Most babies are beautiful. I don't mention his looks to single him out as special, but merely as a visual introduction. It's what's inside that so endears this child to all who know him.

Jarrod is blessed with a naturally sunny disposition. It's such a pleasure to be around him. He laughs gleefully at everything and finds joy in the simplest things. He comes by his disposition honestly. Watching him smile and react so cheerfully to the world lets me relive his mother's childhood.

Not that Jarrod can't throw a full-blown hissy fit when he's overly tired or truly ticked off about something he deems important. I've seen him fling his tiny body on the floor with such drama that you'd think he's in agony.

When he's mad, he wails with such passion that it's impossible not to laugh. When he's wounded in spirit, his face shows such heartbreak that yours breaks in empathy.

But those times are infrequent, and it's not too difficult to coax him back into a good mood with some loving attention.

For the last month, each time he's been asked, "How old are you going to be on your birthday, Jarrod?" he's smiled sweetly and said, "Two."

"No, baby, you're going to be 3," I tell him.

"I don't want to be 3," he says, still smiling. "I'm 2."

There was no changing his mind. It wasn't until that afternoon when I picked him up for some one-on-one time that he finally announced, smiling that sunny smile, "I'm 3!" He crawled into his car seat and as I buckled him in, broke into song: "Happy birthday to me, happy birthday to me..."

"You're such a big boy," I tell him. "No, I'm not," he says in a singsong. "I'm little."

I can't say that I blame him. Although I look forward to watching him grow, I love this stage of childhood. A 3-year-old's personality is so clearly defined. He is articulate enough to express both simple and complex thoughts, keeping you hanging onto each word, trying to get inside his little brain.

But he's still baby enough to let you cuddle and tickle and grab kisses off sweet skin. That time can pass much too soon.

His Uncle Chris was much like Jarrod, wanting kisses and hugs well into childhood. Chris eventually denied me goodbye kisses, given quickly in the car in front of school, when he was 7 and noticed that some other boys didn't kiss their mothers goodbye.

I remember tears welling up as I understood that he'd taken yet another step away from me.

So for now, I gratefully grab Jarrod's kisses and hugs whenever he gives him, holding them tight like so many radiant stars destined to vanish with the dawn.

Marriage
February 10, 2002

When it comes to love, what you don't do or say sometimes is more important that what you do.

Married couples celebrating their first Valentine's Day often have much different expectations than those who are on year No. 5 or 10 or 20.

Newlyweds tend to gather all the romance and promise of their blossoming love and dump the emotional mix onto one little square of the yearly calendar. They are certain that on Feb. 14, their lover-turned-spouse will help create a perfect 24 hours that confirm that yes, indeed, theirs is the most powerful love ever felt.

What an expectation for one mere mortal to fill.

If a spouse doesn't write just the right words on the perfect card, doesn't take his loved one to just the right romantic restaurant (or if she doesn't prepare just the right special dinner), and then fails to present Sweetie Pie with just the right gift, those big old satin and lace hearts that symbolize Valentine's Day are replaced with weepy, wounded ones.

If expectations — unrealistic or otherwise — aren't met, a couple can do one of two things: go with the flow or go into meltdown.

Take some sound advice. Go with the flow.

Marriages that last share at least one strength: they dwell more on what is right than what is wrong. When they quarrel, as all couples will, they either settle the issue or agree to disagree and move on.

One year, my sweet husband brought home a beautiful vase of roses. Something was said or done that quickly escalated into a full-blown argument.

He looked at me with disgust and muttered, "Well, that was a waste of $50."

Boy, was that the wrong thing to say.

"Oh, I see," I thought. The flowers weren't given out of love. They were given to accomplish a personal agenda and he now needs to point out that since I didn't do or say exactly whatever it was he expected, I didn't deserve them in the first place.

I promptly opened the back door and flung the flowers, vase and all, as far as I could, barely missing our startled dog, who ducked and ran for cover. Wise move.

I can't remember what the argument was about. That's the point. Arguments come and go. It's what you do after that matters most.

I called my husband to ask if he remembered what started that battle. He didn't, God bless him.

All he could remember was that he'd said something that sent me right over the edge.

We've been married 21 years. For discussion's sake, let's say we've had at least one good argument a month. That comes to 252 arguments since the day we said our vows.

Would you want to be able to list 252 reasons why you lost your temper or had your feelings hurt?

I hope not.

Strong marriages focus on the day-in, day-out, lifetime commitment we make to each other. The commitment we keep through the tough times as well as the easy.

An unbreakable marriage is one in which we hold onto the dozens of things our spouse does each day that demonstrate love far better than a dozen roses do.

Not that roses are bad.

The first year we were married, my husband kept a fresh rose in a bud vase on my desk at work at all times. I loved those single stems, and what was in his heart when he brought them to me.

These days, however, I'm just as thrilled when he weeds the garden.

One of the best Valentine gifts you could give to your spouse is to pull the weeds from your marriage memory bank, toss them aside to make room for lovely new blooms.

A rose now and then is perfectly acceptable, too.

Love of roses finally blooms
April 28, 2002

I am infatuated, drawn to any magazine with roses on its cover.

I've never considered myself a particular fancier of the rose. For the life of me, I don't know why. Thinking back, I realize that I've had at least one or two rosebushes in every yard of my life.

I'm not a rosarian. I haven't taken very good care of my roses. I bought into the idea that roses are fussy and I made a bargain with mine from day one.

"I'll plant you, water you and maybe feed you once in a while. That's it. The rest is up to you."

I didn't prune them, spray them or coax them into shape.

Instead, I focused my attention on digging out beds and trying various annuals and adding to my stock of perennials. Bulbs are my favorites. Stick them in the ground, walk away and nature does the rest.

The one exception to my apparent lack of affection for roses is my grandmother's rosebush, planted somewhere around the 1930s or '40s, behind the country store she and my grandfather ran in Kingsland, Ark.

I don't know the variety. I know it's a rambler that almost nothing can suppress.

Although the store is long gone, each spring, her rosebush is laden with hundreds, if not thousands, of perfectly formed buds of the palest pink. The bush, now spread into a cascading mound at least 40 feet across, puts on a short-lived show, but oh, what a show it is.

Many of my aunts and my favorite uncle have rosebushes that grew from her cuttings.

I'm on my second or third cutting. Mine never did well. I couldn't decide where to put them in my heavily shaded yard, so I let them lie dormant while I worried about where to plant them, and, fearful of

Ruby Lee Johnson Nowlin

doing the wrong thing, did nothing at all.

This past year, after finally clearing our fence line, I gave the lone survivor a home in the corner of the yard, where it can ramble all it wants.

I have sprayed and watered it well and it's so grateful it already has tripled in size.

For the past two weeks, I have been walking out and touching the deep green leaves and watching the buds form and thinking about how faithful it has been to an unfaithful steward.

I send thoughts of gratitude to my grandmother, not only for the love she nourished me with in life, but for the nourishment she gave a rosebush more than 50 years ago that continues to feed my soul.

I think about how her hands might not have touched these leaves or petals, but planted the roots from which they grew.

And I have utterly surrendered to the romance of cascading, climbing roses, profuse with blooms.

I'm old enough to understand the importance of allowing myself to be seduced by certain things.

If I had my life to live over, I would be one of those people who rescue roses from abandoned farmhouses and homesteads. I'd proliferate them as fast as I could, handing them out to people who would cherish them.

I'd be content with the thought that hundreds of years later, some foolishly romantic woman susceptible to their heady grace would run her fingers over the dark green leaves, bury her face in fragrant blooms, and give thanks.

Thanks, Dad

June 16, 2002

As a child, I dreaded Father's Day.

Each June, teachers were prone to hand out such assignments as "Why My Dad is the Best Dad in the World" or "The Most Important Thing My Father Ever Taught Me."

I never wrote such a paper, since I'd never met my father. I didn't know where he was or even what he looked like. I lived with my grandparents, and since I wasn't close to my grandfather, I didn't have an acceptable substitute.

I was long past childhood when I met my father for the first time. I already had learned how to skip a rock across the surface of a river, how to shoot marbles and how to pull apart a honeysuckle blossom and sip the nectar.

But I still had things to learn.

It's been a long time in the making, but here's the essay I never got to write.

"Things I Learned From (or were confirmed by) My Dad."

Love can lie dormant inside a heart for as long as it takes.

Discovering who we are and what our destiny is sometimes takes a lifetime.

The spirit is easily wounded, but can heal.

No matter what happens later, love given never is wasted.

Laughter, deep and frequent, is critical to the soul.

The only way to keep a bird from flying the coop is to constantly mend the tears in the wire.

If you wait too long to mow the pasture, there will be no daffodils in the spring.

Watching someone have a good time is even better than having it yourself.

Revisit the pleasures of childhood as often as possible.

He reminded me of things I'd almost forgotten, like a homegrown apple is far sweeter than any you can buy and that you can never put too much dill in your pickles.

He taught me that the picture we allow others to paint of us when we are children frequently becomes what we see in a mirror, no matter how old we are.

There are times when you have to do what you have to do and let the chips fall where they may.

Sometimes you have to suck it up and accept that some things will never be the way you want them.

In the five years and three months I spent with my Dad before he

JACK HUNT AND HIS RHYTHM RANCH
HANDS. DAD IS ON THE FAR LEFT.

died, he reinforced a lesson it took me most of my life (and a patient husband) to learn: If someone believes in you strongly enough, you can grow to believe in yourself.

And he taught me this: We all have music in our souls, but many of us go to the grave with it still unplayed.

Not my Dad.

And not me.

Country road pulls home

August 11, 2002

Some time ago, I spent the better part of a day interviewing a man in East Texas who enjoyed doing things the old-fashioned way, like smoking his own hams.

His smokehouse was filled with the scents of my childhood. I walked around the old family log cabin and noted the ground, worn smooth from generations of kids playing and dogs sleeping in the cool shade.

He introduced me to his wife, a frail woman in a thin cotton dress who greeted me warmly.

As I said goodbye later, I noticed the wood-burning stove, worn linoleum floor and plastic dishes in the sink.

I rolled the windows down in the car so I could enjoy the sun and cool, late spring air and drove slowly across the deeply rutted roads. I came to a bend and saw railroad tracks rising ahead.

I stopped, unable to go any further, overwhelmed with a feeling I couldn't describe or understand. The dirt road, the sound of the wind in the pines, the railroad tracks that rose just enough that I couldn't see what was on the other side of them — the sense of place was so strong and so familiar that I didn't want to leave it.

I sat there and wept, overcome with the sense there was a message I couldn't quite grasp. I wanted to understand, but I couldn't, and I was filled with sadness beyond description.

Later, I tried to reason it out. It was like being home, I figured. I was 10 years old again. The thick red dirt, the curve in the road, the railroad track, the sound of the wind — it was exactly the same as the road leading to my childhood home in Arkansas. The woman in her cotton gown made me re-live my grandmother's last months before she died of cancer and the log cabin made me think of Dad — the two people who most would have understood exactly what I was feeling.

I was homesick for a place and time that no longer existed.

Has that ever happened to you? Have you ever had the sense that a time and place long gone are more real, more who you are than the present?

That night, I dreamed that my grandmother was looking for her garden but couldn't find it. I asked where it was. She said she didn't have one. I knew how much she loved her garden and there never had been a time in her life that she didn't have one, so it must be that something beyond her control was keeping her from it.

"Do you want one?" I asked. "Yes," she said. "Then I'll help you," I told her, and we started looking for the best place to dig.

I woke the next morning feeling more at peace, but I still felt as if there was a message I was missing.

I remembered the song I was listening to on that red dirt road the day before and how it stayed with me. It was Gram Parson's "A Song for You."

"Oh my land, it's like a wild goose, wanders all around, everywhere . . . Jesus built a ship to sing a song to, it sails the rivers, it sails the tide. Some of my friends don't know who they belong to; they can't get a single thing to work inside."

For 20 years, I belonged to the woman who loved me and took care of me. And then she died. For five years, I belonged to the father I had looked for all my life. And then he died. And all of a sudden, I couldn't get a single thing to work inside.

I'm 55, and the first two thirds of my life are gone. And sometimes, even now, the place I feel most comfortable is a dusty road by the railroad tracks.

You have to love the 'before' as well as the 'after'

August 25, 2002

Recently, a good friend and I were talking about what attracted us to our husbands.

For her, it was his stability, that constancy of demeanor that said, "It'll all work out."

While she was prone to quick, emotional reactions to change and challenge, he sat back, assessed the situation and then moved forward.

His calming presence kept her level, she said, and feeling that things were under control.

After they were married for a while, she found that levelness of emotion lacking a bit.

"Sometimes," she said, "I wanted to shout, 'Can't you get at least a little excited about this?' "

His constant calmness began to seem more like lack of enthusiasm.

I, on the other hand, was attracted to my mate's energy, excitement and sense of humor. His personality exemplified "joie de vivre," a love of life that was a perfect counterweight to my sometimes too serious, moody self.

After we were married for a while, his energy, teasing and emotional boundlessness sometimes left me gasping for air.

My friend, who has studied social work and counseling, said one of the things she often tells others is this: "When you fall in love, pick out the trait that you like the most and that makes you the happiest. Write that down so you can look at it later and remember how it made you feel, because someday, that same thing will become the thing that annoys you the most. Then, you have to do the work of loving one another to live with it."

The good thing about this, she said, is that you eventually meet in the middle, having absorbed some of the best in each other.

We had a good laugh over how different a trait appears in its "before" and "after" states.

Stable becomes boring. Playful becomes immature. Mature becomes dreary.

Thrifty turns into stingy and generous becomes irresponsible. Attentive becomes smothering and independent becomes aloof. Strong begins to feel like overbearing and tenderness smells slightly of weakness.

Why do we praise a trait, then criticize it?

My husband says it's because women are never satisfied. They marry a man thinking of him as Play-Doh they can reshape, trimming off what isn't quite perfect and adding on what is.

And your point? I say.

The before-and-after view of a mate isn't limited to females, though. I've known guys who adored their attractive, always-the-center-of-attention women when they were dating, then promptly tried to suppress the irrepressible.

These are the same men who love the way their thin wives look, then complain when they sit down at the dinner table expecting roast beef and mashed potatoes and find themselves nibbling on arugula and tofu.

Then again, we often discover our mates have traits that we didn't hone in on in the beginning, but have become prized attributes.

My husband's self-confidence and lack of need for approval from others is a breath of fresh air. His ability to make decisions and move on without looking back is enviable.

I prize his nonjudgmental, tolerant, generous self.

And let me add that I still love his energy and sense of humor. They keep me buoyant on those days when I am in danger of sinking beneath the heavy cloak of self-imposed responsibility.

My big ol' hunk of Play-Doh looks just about right.

There's still some sculpting left to be done on me.

Moondance
October 13, 2002

Every evening about dusk, I stand beneath a canopy of dense, twining vines and wait for the great unfurling.

Earlier this year, long after anyone should be thinking about planting seeds, I discovered the moonflower vine.

The idea of large, fragrant white blossoms opening at night appealed to me. If you are a Southerner who loves magnolias and gardenias, you need a moonvine.

Years ago, a neighbor had given me a couple of seeds, but I eventually lost track of them. So I bought a brand new pack of seeds and planted them (all of them, foolish old woman that I am) by the trellis my husband built for the climbing rose bushes we bought last year.

They do not disappoint.

The vines sprouted within days. Their tiny but sturdy forms reminded me of diminutive prizefighters punching through the dirt.

These are not shrinking violets. They mean business. They reach out and twine around anything that gets in the way.

I love the thick, dark green, heart-shaped leaves, but it is the sturdy flower buds that intrigue me. They begin as a hard knot, growing bigger by the day. It's hard to imagine something so delicate coming from this.

Eventually, they become long spears, tightly twirled. And then, one evening at dusk, you look at the bud and know it is time.

If you are a patient person, you can actually see it happen. That's how anxious these blooms are. You'd think they would make a long, slow dance of unfurling, since they are destined to show their faces only in moonlight. By morning, they will be gone, once again closed in a spiral before falling to the ground.

One blossom. One night.

But there are dozens more where those came from. Each evening, they begin to twirl open, the leaves around them shaking ever so slightly, leaving you wondering if you only imagined it.

Within an hour or so, the partially open blooms are visible, their intense fragrance carried on the night air. As darkness deepens, the flowers completely unfurl into six-inch trumpets that glow in the moonlight.

If I'm late getting home, the ancient trees around my house intensify the darkness. I can barely make out the shape of the fence line and the house, but I can see the big blooms, shimmering in the pale light.

Six weeks ago, I picked the first blossom that opened, captivated by its fragrance. I put it in a tiny cobalt blue vase by my bed, thinking I'd inhale that scent all night.

The moonvine had other plans. It collapsed in a thin sheet and the fragrance vanished.

This is a bloom that dances only for the moon.

One night, as I stood watching the blooms, I heard the rapid beating of wings close by.

A moth bigger than any I'd known was hovering like a hummingbird over a fully opened bloom. He dipped an amazingly long, thin proboscis into the trumpet, drank deeply, then pulled back and moved on.

Although he was barely half an arm's length away, he didn't seem to mind my presence.

The pack of moonvine seeds was only a dollar or two but already has given me pleasure beyond price.

I don't know if the vine will reseed. If so, I might have to curtail its growth so it doesn't overpower the rosebushes that are starting to take off.

But there will always be a place in my yard — and in my life — for a flower that dances for the moon.

Boys and bandages
Oct. 20, 2002

All she said when I answered the phone was, "Mom."

"What's wrong?" I asked.

When you're a mother, you can read your child's voice, even one word spoken over a cell phone with bad reception.

It was Saturday and I was on my way to run errands before I was to meet my firstborn at the pizza place to help celebrate her firstborn's 5th birthday.

While she was mopping up the water her two boys had splashed all over the bathroom floor, they were having a merry old time, running through the kitchen with the wild abandon that only two little heathens, one 3 and one just turned 5, possess.

It was just about then that she heard the thud and the scream.

By the time she got to him, his head and face were covered with blood. She found a deep gash in his scalp where it had connected with the sharp corner of the granite cabinet in the kitchen.

She looked up at the clock and realized it was a half-hour before his big brother's birthday party was to begin.

"Please go to the party and welcome everyone and tell them what happened," she said. "Dad's bringing Jordan. I'll try to get there as soon as I can."

"Do you want me to meet you at the hospital?" I asked. "No," she said, assuring me that she was OK. It was important to her that the guests, some of whom didn't know each other, had someone there to make them comfortable.

She called a half hour later to say it was going to be at least an hour or two before they saw the doctor, but not to worry, the baby was fine. In fact, she was having a hard time keeping him still.

"Please make sure Jordan has a good time for his birthday," she urged.

My heart hurt for her, knowing what a difficult position she was in. Her excited firstborn was about to have a birthday party without his mother present — and her injured baby was about to have his scalp sewn back together.

Having been assured that our youngest grandbaby was OK, I couldn't help but laugh. Boy, was this a familiar scene. There's something about our family and emergency room stitches.

When I was about 11, I was on a visit to my mother's, running through the yard like a wild little heathen when I collided with an overturned lawnmower. One of the blades took a two-inch gash in my leg. When the emergency room doctor started stitching it up, my mother fainted.

Years later, on Christmas morning, my 3-year-old son Chris, who had postponed going to the bathroom so he could play with his new toys, went running full speed and collided with the corner of the cabinet.

In the emergency room, he was a perfect patient, never crying as the doctor stitched him up. His mother didn't do as well.

So, here we were again, a mother and child, one with a wounded body and the other with a wounded heart.

Like his uncle, my youngest grandson had done just great during the stitches. He'd even fallen asleep while they were tying the last couple of knots.

My daughter had some shaky moments before she knew his injury wasn't serious, she admitted. Like me, she tends to be calm when called to be, then collapses when her job is done and someone else has taken over. She'd purposely put on a brave front, knowing that if I knew just how scared she actually was, I'd be overcome with worry.

One thing is for sure. October 12, 2002 is not a day we'll soon forget.

Did I mention that it also was her brother's birthday?

That would be the one with the bathroom gash.

Back-seat driver
November 17, 2002

"No driving for two weeks."

As soon as those words left the doctor's mouth, I knew my sentence had been passed.

It wasn't me who couldn't drive. It was the love of my life, the man whose chauffeur I was about to become.

Every woman who has had to drive her husband around because of circumstances beyond his control knows exactly where I'm headed.

My husband is a wonderful man, generous, kind, loving and

protective, but he is, bottom line here, a man.

With few exceptions, men believe they are ordained by God to drive. In fact, they believe they are given special skills not available to women.

Combine that with the pain-induced grumpiness that having a ruptured disc and compressed nerve can bring, and you've got a real challenge on your hands.

I don't mean to minimize my beloved's pain for a second. It was intense and prolonged, so much so that at times watching him suffer literally made my stomach hurt, but believe me, I had another kind of pain to endure.

Because his pain was centered in his lower back, he couldn't sit or stand. Lying down was the only position that brought some small relief. It was almost a week between the time the doctor saw him and the day of surgery, so I had that time, plus his recuperation period, in which I was The Driver.

It was uggggly.

It began even before I backed out of the driveway.

"You're too close to this side," he said. "Straighten up some."

At the end of the street: "There's a car coming" (as if I couldn't see that for myself).

The first mile down the road: "You're going to want to get in the right lane" (as if I didn't drive this road twice a day, five days a week, and usually once on the weekend, which meant I had a pretty good idea where the exits were).

A little farther down the road: "Why are you going this way? If you go the way I go there aren't as many traffic lights." (Never mind that my way had fewer 18-wheelers and less traffic and his had two places in which drivers have to quickly merge lanes. Silly me. Whatever possessed me to think I should be allowed to choose the route I like best when I'M THE ONE DRIVING!)

And then we entered the parking phase.

"Park in that lot," he said, followed by "Not here. It's too close to that truck. Park back there."

I wanted to park, all right — a sock in his overworked mouth.

Help arrived from, of all places, television relationship guru Dr. Phil, whose program on control issues got my husband's attention. When we talked about it, he was able to grin at his behavior, which was real progress. He did, however, have the need to point out that the person on the show with control issues was A WOMAN.

To his credit, ever since that show he's managed to keep his dictatorial side under control, greatly reducing my stress level.

I love you, Dr. Phil.

My much-improved husband is driving himself now, sooner than the neurosurgeon recommended, but then, the good Doc was not the one driving "My Way" McBride around.

For the right price, he could have been. I was willing to go as high as $100.

Saying good-bye
Feb. 23, 2003

She stood in the middle of a room filled with barrels and boxes, sealed with duct tape and labeled in bold black letters: Books. Clothes. Kitchen.

My friend Myra is so petite that when I hug her, she comes about chest high. In that room, which suddenly felt as empty as the boxes were full, this woman who has more energy and strength than most anyone I know was markedly vulnerable.

For two weeks, she had been packing the trappings of life, preparing to move to California to join her husband, Gene, who secured a good job there.

Living in two different states is no way to nourish a marriage. They'd been doing it for months now, and doing it well, but even two strong people can get tired of such a thing.

We should have expected it, I suppose. But somehow it blindsided me. They've lived here so long we figured it was only a matter of time until Gene was back home, enthroned in his leather chair and holding court with "The Group," the couples Gene and Myra pulled into their circle.

There's a bunch of us.

My husband and I are newcomers to The Group. We first sat in their living room 10 years ago, having gone by to drop something off early one afternoon. We didn't know them well, but by 2 o'clock the next morning, when Myra stood at the kitchen stove fixing us breakfast, we did.

Twelve straight hours with relative strangers will do that to you.

That experience sums up what it's like to be friends with Gene and Myra. Their home is a refuge and their friends their touchstone; they love few things more than sharing life with people whose company they enjoy.

How fortunate we are to be among them.

I'm lousy at good-byes. I'm either mute and distant or weepy and clingy. Sometimes both. It speaks to the selfishness in me, that egocentric thing that makes me want to wail, "What am I going to do without you?"

Not that I'm completely selfish. I genuinely celebrate opportunities for those I care about and excitedly imagine the richness and blessings they can bring.

As I said to a red-eyed Myra, "Think of what a great new adventure you have in store."

But eventually, when the shock is over and it settles in that someone I hold dear is about to relocate 1,500 miles away, I come back to me.

What will it be like not to be able to pick up the phone and say, "Can I come over?" and then show up in my pajamas, as I sometimes have?

In analyzing why we became friends, after running down the list of obvious things: an ease with each other, an appreciation for the ways we are alike as well as the ways we are different and, in the end, an unexplainable need to be friends, it hits me.

They let us be selfish.

In taking care of us, perhaps they also take care of themselves.

There's something in people like them that is most satisfied when they are feeding others, whether it's food or drink or conversation.

The loyalty they've garnered from those whose company they seek speaks to that.

Mowers rule
March 30, 2003

The sun was shining, the birds were singing, the trees waved gently in the cool breeze and the lawn mower called my name.

You know those commercials where the guy gazes proudly at his new lawn mower as he gently strokes the hood? That's me.

The whine of the engine as it attempts to turn over, the hiccups and backfire as it finally starts, the sputtering of the engine and the grind of the transmission — all are music to my ringing ears.

Our lawn mower once looked and sounded like that magnificent red machine in the commercials, except ours is green. Sort of. The sun has long since faded it into a shade resembling overcooked egg yolk.

The original seat is rusting in a landfill somewhere. Long after the vinyl shredded so badly the ridges made for seating challenges, long after the springs had sprung, long past the day the whole seat fell off, we continued to use it.

My husband, being resourceful, had to use heavy plastic tie-downs to anchor it well enough to fool the safety switch. It was a proud moment for me. I've never loved him more.

I'm a practical woman. It is my belief that as long as something runs (my car is up to 176,000 miles), why not use it?

I was a tad worried about the seat falling off while The Spouse was driving it, but he was perfectly happy with the challenge. The real reason he refused to get a new seat was quite transparent. It kept me off it. If it were up to my husband, I'd never touch the lawnmower. It's not that he wants to mow; he sees me as a threat.

To the lawn mower, not to him.

Just because I once drove it up a tree, just because I occasionally run over something that shouldn't be in the wrong place at the wrong time, just because I feel a challenge to get as close to the fence line as I can, he gets grumpy.

He's mentioned a time of two or seven that he'd prefer I not use the lawn mower when he's gone.

I find that rather condescending.

So, if I have an hour or two before sunset and one day before rain is due yet again and the grass is high and he has to work late, well, then, why not make hay while the sun shines?

That's what I told myself earlier this week as I sat there, covered in mud, courtesy of uselessly spinning wheels buried to the rim.

It seems I had located a low spot by the back fence line.

The thought of telling him the lawnmower was buried was not a pleasant one. I tried everything I could think of. I rocked it back and forth. It only sunk deeper. I put some small tree branches under the back wheel for traction. No dice.

I tried boards. No good.

I considered calling my neighbor to come pull it out with his tractor, but I didn't know if I had enough beer to bribe him into keeping quiet.

Besides, I figured tractor tire ruts would be a dead giveaway.

What else could I do? I 'fessed up.

He took it rather well. Maybe he was just glad I hadn't done what one of my friends did with her tractor — brought down a guidewire that brought down a highline that brought traffic on Interstate 10 to a halt.

Luckily, her husband was out at the time, so she called Entergy to make the repair and they were gone by the time he returned. She thought she was home free until he asked, "Did we lose power today?"

She had forgotten to reset the flashing red numerals on all the appliances.

She was so close.

You've got to admire a woman like that.

Section Five

May 25, 2003 to September 26, 2004

THE NOWLIN FAMILY (FROM LEFT, SHIRLEY, BILLY, SUE, GLADYS, JUANITA, HURSHEL, HELEN, BURNICE, RUBY AND TURNER NOWLIN) IN FRONT OF NOWLIN GENERAL STORE IN KINGSLAND, ARKANSAS

Virginia Woolf got it right

May 25, 2003

"I need one of those," my daughter said. She was talking about a plaque hanging over the computer in my home office with these words from Virginia Woolf: "A woman must have money and a room of her own."

The words evidently resonate as clearly with her as they did for me.

I don't remember my grandmother ever having a money talk with me when I was growing up. She didn't give me advice about finances before she died when I was 20, but I observed enough to know that she understood how important it is to a woman to have money "of her own."

Counting my mother, for whom money meant mobility, that's four generations of women in our family who always made sure they had a bit of cash stashed away.

It's not hard to understand why.

My grandmother belonged to a generation and a society in which women had little, if anything to say about money matters. She never held a full-time job outside the home, but she worked harder than my grandfather ever did. She raised a garden with a mule and a plow, canned food, cooked three meals a day (on an old iron stove for most of her life), milked a cow and churned her own butter, raised chickens for eggs and meat, kept house, brought water in from a well for all the household needs, washed clothes in a tub with a scrub board and raised eight children.

The only pay she received was the satisfaction of knowing she was feeding and caring for her family.

If my grandmother needed something, she had one of two choices: ask my grandfather for the money or find another way. Only a woman who has had to ask her husband for money for her every need understands the dependency and sense of devaluation that brings.

My grandmother never had much and expected less. My grandfather never allowed her to learn to drive, so unless her destination was close enough to walk, she was dependent on him to take her to town.

She found ways to earn a little money, from selling eggs, milk and butter to picking cotton. She was 40 years old when her last child was born. She spent that day in the fields, earning 1 to 2 cents a hundred, or somewhere around 50 cents a day.

Because money was so precious, she guarded it well. She carried it in a cotton Bull Durham tobacco bag with a drawstring top, about the size of a pack of cigarettes, fastened to the inside of her dress with a safety pin. It wasn't the money she was focused on. It was the security it gave her.

Ma taught her girls to take care of themselves. Raise a garden, can your food or freeze it, she told them. It's like money in the bank. Some years, she put up 400 to 500 jars, from fruit to vegetables and even meat when she could.

They learned well. It was not her husband, but her daughters who bought her an electric churn and a water pump to bring water inside the house.

In her later years, she took to hiding money around the house. When she was dying of lung cancer, she told my Aunt Burnice, "The Dahlia bulbs are yours."

When my aunt dug them up, as you do with dahlias each year, she found a can with valuable old coins buried beneath them.

During her last week of life, when she was coherent, she kept whispering to me about money and where it was. She didn't want something she struggled so hard to get to go to waste.

It wasn't easy for my grandmother, but she made sure she had money she could call her own. Her "room" was her garden, where she sought both solace and substance.

We, her daughters and granddaughters and great-granddaughters, understand that so well.

Family ties never unravel
June 1, 2003

We sat in a circle on a tree-shaded deck, nine tired but exuberant bodies in chairs pulled close.

Since I graduated from high school in 1965 and moved to Texas, I've been back to visit my family in rural Arkansas many times, but this was a first.

Three aunts, an uncle, two cousins and a dear high school friend had made the seven-hour trip to visit me. For some of them, it was their first time in Texas; for all of them, it was their first look at my world as it is now.

For four days, they wandered room to room, looking at the trappings of a post-Arkansas life they knew little about.

They picked up the hundred or more framed photos scattered about and exclaimed happily over pictures of family members.

"You really made this?" my cousin Wanda asked about a quilt, eyebrows raised in her "don't-lie-to-me" look. I don't know why she had such a hard time believing it. I guess in her mind I'll always be the scattered adolescent who avoided household chores, preferring to play outside.

They walked the yard and catalogued my plants, especially my Aunt

Shirley, who, like me, inherited my grandmother's love of flowers.

They gathered in the kitchen, efficiently helping prepare meals, setting the table and cleaning up. It was as if they had been there a hundred times.

Mostly, we talked. We talked about our lives now and we remembered days past. We laughed and laughed and, when we thought we were all laughed out, laughed some more.

We shed a few tears, too.

My family was extraordinarily close growing up. My grandparents, with whom I lived all my life and who later adopted me, treated me like their ninth child. My Aunt Shirley, the baby of the family, is only 6 years older than I am, so I might as well have been.

Leaving home at 17 and starting a new life in another state, by its very nature, changed that.

It didn't diminish the love or closeness in mind and spirit, but it did in body. I no longer could walk next door and see my aunt and cousins. I no longer spent Saturdays, Sundays or summers with aunts and uncles whose homes were like my own.

When Wanda first told me she, Shirley and Uncle Billy were coming to visit, I was elated. When she called a few days later and said, "When everybody found out we were going to your house, they said, 'I want to go, too.' So I guess we're just going to have a family reunion," I was ecstatic.

I was especially pleased that her best friend from high school, Mary Nell, was coming. I'd gladly have taken a dozen more.

It wasn't like the old days, when my grandmother would pull out mattresses and throw them on the floor and make quilt pallets to sleep 15 or 20, but it was almost as good.

A house full of family makes for full hearts, and mine was overflowing.

Nothing feels better than sharing time with people to whom you are linked, not only by blood, but also by love.

I wish you could have seen us, talking and laughing and hugging and drinking in the blessing of being together, but I know you know exactly what I'm talking about.

I'm just glad you weren't there to see the good-byes. You'd have bawled right along with me.

My family left behind a cluster of thoughtful gifts: a fragrant gardenia bush, a lacy hydrangea, a lovely picture frame and a cross.

As much as I will cherish those, my favorite gift required a different expenditure.

My family gave me their time, and that bought precious, precious memories.

Atticus Finch

June 15, 2003

She sat upright in the waiting room chair, perfect posture, perfect hair, perfect composure.

There were a lot of us there, waiting in a medical office for our names to be called.

As friendly people are wont to do, she struck up a conversation with the woman in the chair next to her. I was three seats down and across, close enough to easily hear the conversation.

She was retired, the attractive older woman said to her waiting-room neighbor, but busy trying to find a renter for one of the apartments she owned.

More accurately, she added, she was busy trying to decide who the lucky renter would be.

"I'm very picky about who I rent to," she said.

She went on to say how the neighborhood where the apartment is located is all white, and she certainly wasn't going to be the first one to rent to a black.

"I couldn't do that to those people," she said, then added with a casualness that took my breath away, "I'll burn them down first."

It's not as if I haven't heard such statements before. But it's been many years and in very different settings.

I looked up, stunned by the fact that she hadn't dropped her voice to a whisper, hadn't looked around to see who might be listening, hadn't given any indication that what she was saying would be of interest or taken exception to, let alone possibly offend or wound, any of the 20 or more people within earshot.

She continued the conversation with barely a pause, moving on to topics banal and insignificant, until she was called to the back.

For the next hour, people rose and left, entered and sat, a constantly changing still life.

Just a few minutes after the first woman had left, an equally elegant woman with skin the color of sable took her seat.

The woman and her male companion carried on a quiet conversation, just as others around them did.

It was as if the whole incident never had happened.

Barely 30 minutes before, I had listened to a different conversation as a woman sitting across from me responded to a question about the book she was reading.

The woman explained that she was an English teacher and was re-reading a familiar favorite that was being placed on the reading list for her students.

The book was Harper Lee's "To Kill a Mockingbird."

In that waiting room, acutely aware of the bitter irony of the moment and immersed in the sadness of it, I lost some of the optimism that I cling to as a Southerner, the earnest belief that we are not the people we once were.

I hold no false belief that prejudice has been eradicated. I feel certain it never will be.

But, as someone who speaks up when non-Southerners lump us into one backward bunch of racists, my spirit was broken.

Thursday, as I sat and pondered all the sub-text of that conversation, I heard about the death of Gregory Peck, the actor who portrayed a man whose quiet strength and courage had been one of the strongest influences of my adolescence.

The sense of loss I felt was acute.

If I had been able to sit down and talk with him at that moment, I just know Atticus Finch would have been able to offer words of wisdom and encouragement. He would have helped me make sense of the senseless.

I know Atticus Finch was a character from a movie and a book, but he was real to me, as was everything he represented.

And I think about all of us who believed in him, and in others like him, and who now mentally rise in respect, because Atticus Finch is passing.

'Sleeps'
Aug. 17, 2003

The photograph shows a barefoot boy of 4, wearing a white T-shirt and short overalls. His right hand, the one he uses for writing but not for eating, is tucked inside a pocket. He leans on his left elbow and rests chubby toes on a small stepladder, striking the perfect studio pose.

It's one of my favorite pictures of Jordan, one of the last before he began to weary of having his picture taken. These days, he's more likely to cross his arms and purse his lips in protest or, on good days, strike an absurd pose with a fake grin.

That was two years ago, when our adored first grandchild still walked in that shifting sand between the blissful contentment of toddlerhood and an awakening awareness of the world outside himself, a world that held expectations that sometimes collided with his own.

Jordan was born an aged soul. He's always been a little too serious for his Grammie, who would like to see him cling to carefree frivolity and innocence as long as possible.

He's a thinker, this child who holds far more in his head and heart than he is willing to release, even to his Mom, who watches him wistfully and wonders about those things he's holding close.

Each evening, she asks about his day. He sometimes reports on something of significance, but more often than not, gives a one or two-word answer and then moves on. If he's not interested in sharing, no amount of coaxing or coaching will change that.

So we who love him take those moments, store and savor them.

For weeks now, our little man has been counting "sleeps."

For Jordan, who has trouble mastering the nuances of time, a "sleep" is one day. That means he'll go to bed and when he awakens, it has been one sleep. Two days are two sleeps. Trying to count much beyond that dissolves into the intangible.

The reason Jordan has tried to keep such careful count of his sleeps lately is this: a day so monumental that even a 5-year-old grasps its importance.

Late last week, he told me, "Grammie, in 10 more minutes, I'm going to kindergarten."

"No," I told him, "not 10 minutes."

Before I could get another word out, he loudly protested. "Yes, it is. My Mom said I'm going to kindergarten in 10 more minutes."

If Mom says it, it is so.

"Baby, it's not 10 minutes," I said. "I think you mean 10 days."

He fell silent.

OK, I could sense him reasoning. That makes sense. Maybe she's right.

At that point, it was only a few days, not 10, but that was beside the point. It was coming up.

It came much too soon.

Every parent and grandparent knows the feeling of being torn between the pleasure of sharing in a child's movement from one experience to another and the grieving for days left behind. Days that cannot be retrieved, only remembered.

Still, I love the opportunities each new day brings with this child, because I so love interacting with him.

I count as blessings those times when I can engage him in conversations on things he finds worth pondering — and I am in constant pursuit of such things.

This past week, Jordan's world grew immeasurably larger.

And if I am wise enough to display just the right amount of interest, carefully tempered with patience, I might receive an invitation into a fragile place, one so momentary and worth cherishing.

In far too few sleeps, it will be gone.

Don't touch that handle
August 24, 2003

I've decided it's time to go public about public toilets. I'm a foot flusher.

Yes, I'm one of those germ-wary, prissy souls who evidently took it as gospel the first time I saw one of my female relatives plant her feet and do the squat-and-hover.

Never mind that we lived in the country and some of us still had outhouses that exposed us to much worse than we were likely to encounter in the downtown service station. We were, by gosh, citified enough to known that a lady never allowed her derriere to touch a public toilet seat.

Heaven only knows what unwashed heathen might have sat there, leaving behind horrible things we could only imagine. While I heard and heeded dire warnings from my germ-obsessed Aunt Helen about all the micro-organisms in the world searching for the perfect host, for me, it became more about ick than sick.

Not only do I hover and hoof, I also pre-plan.

When I am forced to use a truly repulsive-looking bathroom, I get my paper towel before I wash my hands so I don't have to put clean hands on dirty knobs and dispensers — duh — and after I've used it to turn off the water and dry my hands, use it to open the bathroom door.

Go ahead and laugh. As my 4-year-old grandson Jarrod says when I tell him he looks silly clomping around in his mother's stilettos, "I don't care."

Of course, I rest in the perfect assurance, if not comfort, that I am far from alone in my lack of affection for public privies.

A Newhouse News Service story recently said that, when it comes to distaste for public rest rooms, there's really not that much difference between women and men.

Yeah, right.

Not that I think men are indifferent to dirt. It's just that I assume women are more likely to go overboard about such things, while men have a rather, ummm, healthier attitude.

So I asked around.

I wish you could have seen the abject terror on the faces of some of my male co-workers when faced with the question, "Have you ever flushed a toilet with your foot?"

No man ever answers a question like that without running it through his Man-O-Meter.

The first one tentatively said, "Yes." The second one looked at me as if I were setting a trap. The third, God bless him, didn't hesitate.

"You bet I have."

I asked another coworker if he avoided public rest rooms. He said it depended on whether his knees had to bend.

Do a little 'Net surfing and you'll find all sorts of products for public toilet use, from slip-on sleeves to, I kid you not, a folding toilet seat that goes on the permanent toilet seat. It even has its own shoulder bag to "assure you of easy, inconspicuous handling."

I say if you're going to carry around a portable toilet seat, being conspicuous is not your biggest concern. Even though the seat comes with a disinfectant spray bottle, what self-respecting germ hater (the obvious customer) is going to want to put that seat back into the bag after it's been used?

Just in case you were wondering, there's no money-back guarantee.

I leave you non foot-flushers with this thought: You know all that filthy stuff on some public rest room floors? Someone just transferred it to the handle of the commode you're about to flush.

And to my fellow foot-flushers, maybe we should be more considerate. Instead of using our foot, we could use a protective barrier of toilet paper to flush instead.

Then, toss it and hurry outside so you can wipe your shoes on the carpet.

Even bruised hearts can be grateful

November 23, 2003

Give thanks with a grateful heart . . .

These familiar words will fall at countless gatherings today when we as a country prepare for Thanksgiving, and as individuals, reflect on our lives.

Remembering to count blessings and cultivating a thankful heart are recurring themes in my life and because of that, appear in these conversations we share each week.

It is my sincere belief that we all have something for which we can be grateful and yes, I urge you to do just that.

But it also is important to acknowledge that there are times when we just don't feel grateful. And that's OK.

I think that's worth repeating, because it's one of two thoughts I hope you take away today.

It's OK sometimes not to feel particularly grateful.

This has been a difficult year. I've watched those around me endure losses that left them shaken and bereft. When life changes in the span of days, hours or even minutes, it can leave us feeling as if life is out of control. That's because it is.

For many of us, that's a hard thing to accept. We like to think that if we take care of business, things will go pretty much as we expect, or as we hope. Yes, we acknowledge that we can't control everything around us — we're not stupid, after all — but inside, where our comfort lives, we hold out hope that we can keep things evenly balanced.

The reality is, we cannot.

We have no way of knowing what will happen from one moment to the next. When the things that happen are unexpected or uninvited, we are shaken.

We try to live each day with a certain amount of confidence and faith. Confidence that we are prepared to tackle whatever comes our way and faith that we will survive it.

On some days, we don't feel like survivors. We become shell-shocked casualties of a conflict not of our choosing. Where confidence was, insecurity takes hold.

People we love die. People we love don't love us. People behave in ways that we don't understand.

Our health fails, our income drops or disappears and relationships weaken or dissolve.

None of us will escape this reality. No matter how blessed our lives have been, at one time or another, we will be asked to endure disappointment, pain and loss.

Life is the great leveler. It will have its way with us.

And when it does, we have a decision to make. Where do we go from here?

Do we grieve? Yes. Should we expect time to mourn for what we've lost? Yes.

Do we seek the comfort and counsel of those whose wisdom we value? By all means.

But then, it's time to go on.

That's the second point I hope you take away. Life demands much of us. It frequently asks things we'd rather not give.

No matter how impossible it seems, no matter how badly bruised our hearts and hopes are, we can encourage each other with the knowledge that this too, shall pass.

It may not pass as quickly as we want, or in the manner we want, and for a while, we might not feel very grateful.

But if we want it to, if we work for it, it will.

And we again can give thanks with a grateful, healed heart.

Orderly world is secure

February 1, 2004

"Grammie, you weren't supposed to pick me up today."

Standing in the middle of his daycare classroom, our oldest grandchild fixed his gaze on me, eyebrows furrowed.

He wasn't displeased with the idea of going home with me. The difference between his usual greeting — an excited, "Grammie!" — and this one was his displeasure with something being changed without his knowledge.

"Mom is supposed to pick me up," he said.

I explained that his mom didn't know when she dropped him off that morning that his Poppie and I would be asking at the last minute if we could have them overnight. Otherwise, I assured him, she would have let him know.

When he saw his mother the next day, the first thing he said was, "Mom, you're supposed to tell us who's going to pick us up."

He told her this in the most serious of voices, sounding for all the world like a parent scolding a child, a clear indication of the old soul we've all come to recognize.

The conversation was more than a year ago, and everything since has reinforced that this is a child who craves order.

As a child of divorce, he learned that there are things in his life, big things, which he cannot control or count on staying the same.

For Jordan, adjusting means grabbing hold to all the things he could count on. Like knowing who would come to take him home.

This is a child to whom one doesn't make promises lightly. He will claim them with an acuity that can be sobering to those whose personalities lean more toward taking things as they come.

Both those things matter tremendously to this little boy with the serious eyes and introspective nature.

While his younger brother is as carefree and flexible as a child can be, Jordan demands more.

He insists on knowing what is going to happen, when it is going to happen and how it will happen. He then commits those things to memory. And that's just the way it had better play out.

Starting kindergarten this year was a momentous challenge. The first few weeks were rocky as Jordan learned to adjust to a world that changed almost daily.

New kids entering his life. A new teacher controlling his day. New rules.

He learned to pay attention to such instructions as "make good decisions," "listen carefully" and "keep your hands and feet to yourself," usually because he hadn't.

Jordan can be singular minded. While he sometimes has trouble listening to instructions, when he is focused on something that interests him, it takes the patience of Job to dislodge him. That ability to fixate on things he wants is going to be of tremendous help later in life, though it occasionally drives us to distraction.

From the time he was a toddler, Jordan has entered a room by looking around and making note of anything that has been moved, added or taken away. Nothing escapes his scrutiny.

This year has ushered our precious little boy into a new room of life, one with which he daily becomes more familiar. All too soon, that too, will change.

But Jordan, we can promise you this: there will always be someone you know and trust, someone who loves you with singular focus, there to pick you up.

Plenty of love to go around
February 8, 2004

The heart's infinite capacity for love is astonishing, don't you think?

While some people lament overuse of the word, thinking it lends a casualness that destroys the integrity of the emotion, it's awfully hard to place a limit on love.

Love will have its way with you.

While I understand the difference between like and love, when I say I love a good cheesecake, believe me, I mean it.

I love my husband, my children, my grandchildren and my siblings. I love my aunts and uncles and cousins, nieces and nephews and dear friends. I love my dog, Annie.

I love two-part harmony, daffodils and perfectly crafted lyrics and prose.

I love the spirited and heartfelt discussions in our Sunday school class.

I love the sure sound of my brother David's fingers against guitar strings, the honesty of his voice and the quiet way he encourages those who love music but lack confidence.

As an adult, I've confided that in childhood I often felt unloved and unlovable. That sorrow shaped the person I became and how I interacted with others, often with hurtful results.

How I wish I had understood that it is futile to chase after love, desperately flailing about in an openhanded and openhearted attempt to snatch it from the very air.

As a middle-aged woman, I've come to recognize that love surrounded me, as it does us all. The anger, hurt and fear that often incapacitated those most in control of my life created a brokenness that prevented me from reaching it.

The carefully kept family secret surrounding my paternity held the power to cripple my sense of self, then restore it later in life when I found my father.

While I love my mother, I didn't live with her growing up and never have been able to develop the kind of relationship I'd like.

The determination to make sure my children never felt distanced from me drove the way I parented and often drove my children to distraction.

As a young mother and divorcee, in an attempt to reassure myself that I was doing things right, I constantly sought signs that my children loved me best. Of course I wanted them to love their dad, just as long as my hold on their heart was stronger.

How much better it would have been for all of us had I known then, as I do now, that a heart's ability to love must be unfailingly nourished and encouraged, not diminished by the foolish and selfish needs of those with some misguided notion of their role in its occupancy.

Listen to me now, those of you whom life has bruised and who haven't yet come to understand how precious a creation you are. When those who love you also love someone else, it does not mean your place in their hearts has been usurped.

You can teach your child few lessons more important than this. Love freely. Love often.

A love given without reservation is not dependent on what happens once it has been released.

Just love.

My husband and I will have been married for 24 years this December. Daily, I learn important things about love from someone who loves unreservedly. The constancy that he extends to our grandchildren, and to me, have taught me more about the workings of the heart than anything else I've known.

His actions speak with more power than any words I could craft, no matter how honest and heartfelt.

How blessed I am to be in the presence of such love.

Yep, that's my daughter
June 6, 2004

My daughter invited me to a party at her home tonight.

At 36, she is a charmer, a complex and beautiful young woman who has passed from young adulthood into a world that asks much more of her than youthful dreams.

At 19, I was married. At 20, I was carrying the child I believed would mark my transformation from girl to woman.

I'd always believed I was destined to be a mother. I knew it. Accepted it. Gave thanks for it.

I had the arrogance, God help me, of one whose naivete allows no room for doubt. Who knows that she is to create, nurture and then release to the world a complete being, unlike any other.

What would there be of me in this new creature? I wondered. Would she have my hazel eyes? Fair skin? Would she love gardening and being immersed in nature?

From childhood, I knew what would happen with my life. I would find a man whose heart beat only for me. A man whose genes would merge with mine and produce something unlike anything that had existed before.

The marriage did not last, but it brought a daughter and a son.

And later, I would find the man whose heartbeat matched mine.

So here I am, sitting in my firstborn's kitchen, watching the girl/woman hostess a holiday weekend party for her friends.

As I watch her refilling wine glasses, replenishing food and introducing newcomers to the group, it hits me.

I am watching myself.

My daughter, God love her, has frequently lamented the fact that it is futile to deny she is my child.

"Mirror, mirror, on the wall," she laughs to her friends, "I am my mother after all."

She is in constant motion, trying to make sure everyone's needs are met.

Her friends turn to me and say, "She's so busy being the perfect hostess. Make her stop."

I laugh, knowing I have as much chance of keeping her from being who she is as I do of changing her eyes from brown to hazel or her skin from olive to cream.

The scene is as familiar as the sound of my own breath.

When I catch her still for a moment, I drape my arms over her shoulders.

"Look around," I tell her, pointing to the corner where three men are engaged in an animated discussion, then to the table, where four vibrant young women are laughing.

"See this," I tell her. "This is what matters. Now slow down and enjoy it."

But I know better. She will look around, take it in, give thanks, then busy herself again with the business of being a hostess.

The years flood back, shocking me with the familiarity. I am in my kitchen, checking to see what I can do to make sure the people who have gathered there are enjoying themselves. I am a blur of motion, moving from kitchen to dining table, placing food and pouring drinks and making sure the music is right.

The music. It is the heartbeat of my life. And now, hers.

I stop and listen. Astonished, I realize that what I hear is "my" music, the music of her childhood. It took a while, but, thanks be to

God, she has come around. And miracle of all miracles, her friends are grooving to it.

She notices me laughing, then says to her friends, "At least I come by it honestly."

I try not to burden my daughter with expectations. I try to encourage her to be her own person.

I needn't have worried.

As much of me as there is in this spectacular young woman, she never was a copy.

Thank God for answered prayers — and prayers answered with wisdom greater than our own.

My daughter invited me to a party. I'm so glad I came.

Spiderman, he isn't

August 15, 2004

Within the first year after moving to the country, my husband and I rediscovered the many joys of rural life.

We became the proud owners of a 90-year-old farmhouse surrounded by trees that cast off limbs, leaves and seeds as carelessly as a child discards clothes.

We inherited a long box of a fence covered with deceitful vines that gently waved delicate fronds about during the day, then doubled madly in size each night, sending out sticky tentacles that threatened to envelop anything that didn't move fast enough. They are so ravenous you would not be surprised to wake up one morning to find a large, green, squirming lump where the dog lay down for the night.

We learned about septic systems that belch and drool and power failures that sweep across the community at the mere suggestion of a thundercloud.

Among the other secrets rural life holds close to its heart are bugs.

Bugs do not alarm me. I do not fear snakes, frogs or crawly things, with the exception of scorpions, which I am convinced are born as Satan stalks to and fro on Earth, looking for the weakest — and the strongest — among us.

With each exhale, drops of his spittle fall to earth as scorpions.

I don't even mind spiders. We've got tiny black ones that are so delicate the breeze generated when someone walks by can send them tumbling. There are moderate-sized ones, with thick bodies and stumpy legs that curl tightly as they back into a crevice and await their prey.

Others range from skinny types with legs so fragile they look as if they couldn't support the spider's body if they didn't come in sets of eight, to chunky ones that could do with a few less carbs.

And then there are the banana spiders.

They are everywhere, clever gigantic arachnids with colors that explode in the morning light. Ours build intricate golden communities around the lamps on our decks, knowing that at night, moths and other foolish flying creatures will throw themselves at the glowing bulbs, only to become the next spiderburger.

These are the spiders that are scaring the bejeebers out of our 6-year-old grandson.

Jordan has no use for anything with hairy legs. While he tolerates the tiny inside spiders that pop up now and then in the far corners of the ceiling, he cannot abide banana spiders.

The first time he came face-to-face with one, he shrieked. We quickly swept away the nest, while I gave him my One With The Earth talk about peaceful co-existence.

"Kill it!" he insisted.

"No," I told him. "It won't hurt us. It's scared of us. It just wants a bug or two to munch on. You're much too big."

Meanwhile, Jarrod, our 5-year-old grandson, was loving it. The minute he realized he had something on his big brother, he leaned in, and in a singsong voice, chanted, "Jordan's scared of spiders, Jordan's scared of spiders."

"Un Uh," Jordan said, ducking his head. "I used to be. Not any more."

Now, when we arrive home with the boys and pull under the carport, before he opens the car door, Jordan peers through the window and asks, "Grammie, did you get rid of the spiders?"

"Yes," I assure him. "They're gone."

A week or two ago, when the boys came over to spend the night, Jordan went on spider patrol, looked at my husband, sighed and grumbled, "Poppie, you need to get another house. This one is too old."

"But we like our house," Poppie told him. "Don't you like it out here, with the big yard and the water garden and the trees?"

"Yes, but Poppie, this house is so old. You could get a new house, close to us. This one has too many spiders."

So we compromised.

We remain in this old house, and regularly sweep unwanted guests away, praying with each stroke that spiders will be the scariest thing this precious boy ever has to face.

Family cherishes little angel
August 22, 2004

My daughter held out her hand and dropped a stack of pictures into mine, radiating a decidedly self-satisfied smile. She positioned herself so she could enjoy my reaction, watching my face as I looked at each one.

They took my breath away, as she knew they would.

I'm considered the photographer in our family, though I think I'm being edged out. I'm known for capturing nice candid shots of family members and have even been roped into taking wedding photos a time or two.

But these pictures were as good as ... OK, better than ... anything I've taken.

It helps to have superb models.

I know you've heard this before, but my grandbabies are breathtakingly, absurdly, heartbreakingly beautiful.

I have two favorite shots. The first is of Jordan and Jarrod on the first day of school. They look like models for Gap Kids, with colorful clothes, new, unscuffed-for-one-day shoes and backpacks. Their hair is perfectly gelled and spiked, and they are beaming, quite pleased with themselves.

The second one is of Jarrod and me, a tight close-up of us leaning in together.

To say I do not like being photographed is a gross understatement. But, oh, this one is a keeper. I love it because both of us are smiling so hard it looks as if our faces will explode. One look at our shared coloring, smiles and cheekbones confirms this is blood of my blood, heart of my heart.

His brother is equally mine, no less beautiful, no less cherished, but in a generous and loving act of wisdom that secured their individuality, God created Jordan to reflect more of his father's side of the family. Like his dad, he will be a handsome man, with olive skin and eyes and a beautifully sculpted face.

The other reason I love this photo is it was taken outside a restaurant where we met to have breakfast before Jarrod went off to kindergarten. It is a momentous day, and the photo marks it well.

When I wrote about Jordan's first day a year ago, I remarked on his old soul in a child's body.

Jarrod is all child. A joyous, exuberant soul who sees the world as a magical place worth exploring — and he doesn't want to miss a moment of it. He doesn't walk. He bounces, or skips or swings from side to side in an exaggerated dance, lost in the sheer pleasure of movement.

There's another photo I love, taken the first day of school this past year. Jordan is dressed and ready to go, smiling for the camera, while Jarrod's face is scrunched and red as he wails and throws himself on the floor, heartbroken at being left behind.

This year, Jarrod channeled his anticipation by marking off the days on the calendar. When they weren't going by fast enough, he and his brother took matters in their own hands and X-ed out four or five at a time.

Who would have thought that the day he'd so looked forward to he would walk into the school with a death grip on his mom's hand?

He took one look around and, sobbing, begged, "Mom, please don't leave me. Please take me home."

His mom hung around in the hall long enough to know he had stopped crying and wasn't going to have a complete meltdown, then went on to work, no doubt whispering the same prayer we do, that Jarrod will love school, do well and make friends — and that his teacher will see into his precious heart and love him, too.

We understand that she has a whole roomful of angels in her care.

But this one is ours.

Time helps us see more clearly
September 26, 2004

The post-surgery call from a doctor 500 miles away helped put my heart at ease.

The arteries of my mother's heart are fragile. A few years ago, doctors tried to counteract the damage by bypassing five arteries.

"It's a miracle she hasn't dropped dead of a massive coronary," the doctor told us, drawing a diagram of her repaired heart.

He didn't get to finish the job because, as my mother likes to say when she's telling the story, "That's when I died on him."

That's pretty much what happened. The doctor had to leave one artery still clogged. Tests showed previous heart damage. Mother's had at least one heart attack, plus several mini-strokes and one serious one.

My mother is a force to be reckoned with. If you don't believe her eight children, just ask the nurses at the Arkansas Heart Hospital. I've seen them try to change her mind about something. It ain't pretty.

By the time her blood pressure shoots to a dangerous level, the nurses start backing off, glancing at me with dismay. I lift my hands and shrug my shoulders. When Mother is in that state, there is no reasoning with her.

The last "Do something" look I got from her nurses came this summer when they asked about medications. Mother read from a list written in her spidery script. When the nurse asked what some of them were, she tensed up. When the questions kept coming, she became agitated. The nurse explained they needed to give the right pills.

That's OK, she told them. She had her pills with her and knew when to take them.

The nurse explained they were required to administer meds.

No, Mother said.

When the nurse took a deep breath and opened her mouth, I held my breath.

"I don't give a damn what your rules are," Mother said, face reddening. "I'm not taking them and if you don't like it . . ."

When the nurse fled in defeat, Mother calmed down. I gently eased into conversation, sitting on the bed and holding her hand, mostly so she couldn't smack me.

"Janie," she said, voice shaking, "I can't tell them what the pills are if

I can't remember." She looked away for a long moment, then back at me, eyes red, shamed with the bitterness of that confession.

This from a woman who worked hard all her life. Still works, with diminished muscle capacity, sitting with an elderly woman at night.

She's taken to asking me the questions she finds hard to ask her surgeon. Anyone who's had surgery knows conversations come back in disjointed bits and pieces, like one of those dreams in which you only feel awake. It's like a puzzle in which the most important pieces are missing, leaving you with an unrecognizable image.

Mother called me Wednesday. After dancing around inconsequential topics, she got down to it.

"Did the doctor tell you I don't have long to live?"

"No, Mother," I told her, taken aback. "Is that what he told you?"

"No."

Fear is a terrible thing. It leaves you shaken and vulnerable, makes you go places you don't want to go.

My mother and I have a complicated history. We've woven a relationship slowly, thread by tenuous thread.

When Mother gets mad, she stops talking to you for months at a time. That hasn't happened the last few years. I think she's loath to waste time.

The puzzle that is my mother is coming together, piece by piece. Although there are gaps, it's no longer an unrecognizable image.

I see a more complex, complete woman. I hope she does, too.

Section Six

October 3, 2004 to August 7, 2005

JANE AND GLORIA

Jane McBride

Two dresses & two sisters

Oct. 3, 2004

There's something not quite right about purple pants.

This is what I think as I stand at the ironing board pressing them. Actually, the pants are lilac, but that's splitting hues. It's a soft, pretty shade, one that looks very much at home on an African violet but not on the backside of a middle-aged woman.

There was a brief time when I coveted all things feminine, as a 12-year-old tomboy who recently discovered the worldview that there is, indeed, a difference between girls and boys.

In retrospect, it wasn't the "them" and "us" discovery that led to a fling with girlie stuff. That came courtesy of my Mean Big Sister.

It was the year our mother gave us new dresses for Christmas. She brought them all the way from Texas to my grandmother's house in Arkansas, where I lived. A new dress was significant. My Aunt Burnice made most of my clothes. Today, I can appreciate the time she spent on something nice for me to wear. Back then, all I saw was "homemade."

A store-bought dress meant I could be like the girls at school who wore department store finery.

We put our dresses on and turned toward each other. My Mean Big Sister, who, despite being two years older was almost a foot shorter, twirled in a circle, holding out the skirt of the most beautiful dress I'd ever seen. It was a soft cream, covered in strawberries, with a full skirt that billowed as she walked.

My dress was a beige sack that hung on my skinny frame.

I hated it.

I looked at my sister's dress, looked at mine and fell silent. I took it off and tossed it on the bed.

I've never been good at hiding my feelings. It has been a curse. I can't get away with anything. What I was very good at was sulking. When my feelings were hurt, I would retreat to nurse my wounds, replaying the scene, which only served to keep the wound raw.

Of course, it wasn't the dresses. In my mind, the beauty of her dress and the ugliness of mine were a reflection of our status in our mother's heart.

At some point, they figured out that I was not thrilled. I told my Mean Big Sister that I liked her dress better. She just smiled. Mother was not happy.

"What's wrong with your dress?" she said.

"It's not pretty like hers."

Mother explained that my dress was "sophisticated," a nuance lost on the likes of me. How could anyone think a baggy beige dress was better than the peaches and cream mound of lace and ruffles?

"Besides," Mean Big Sister said in a snotty voice, "you can't wear feminine things. You're too big. They're for petite girls."

So there it was. Not only was I skinny and clumsy, as my Mean Big Sister had pointed out many times, but I was ugly.

I went straight from hurt to mad. I wanted to pound her and that pretty little dress into the dirt.

It was a fleeting thought. Two things stood in my path.

My choice of reading materials had put me well on my way to developing a pacifist philosophy — and I was and still am a coward.

So I went to be by myself and cried while I tried to figure out why God made me tall, skinny, and ugly and my sister petite and feminine and pretty.

As I unplugged the iron and draped the purple pants across the bed, that memory reminded me of the power of labels. Not the kind that reveal the content of a garment, but the ones that reveal our insecurities.

Is this really how the world sees us?

While they might fade with time, the stitches that hold those labels to us can survive long into adulthood.

Especially when they come from a Mean Big Sister who, by golly, ought to know better.

Life can throw us a challenge or two
October 31, 2004

It's impossible to say which comes first: the shock or the fear.

They exist in equal measure, dark companions that leave you shaken.

Life becomes a waiting game. You wait for the appointment with the surgeon, then wait for the call with the results of the biopsy, even though you know what it's going to be.

You're a journalist. You've researched the words lifted from the radiologist's report: "ill-defined cluster of calcifications."

It will be the first phrase you write in your cancer journal.

Hearing that you have breast cancer is a cakewalk compared to telling those who love you. You wait for the right time and the right words. There are none.

In that horrible, unguarded moment when the words land, the fear on their faces pierces your heart. You decide to tell the rest of your family and friends later, after you get a better handle on what you're facing.

You wait to see an oncologist, anxious to hear how long it will be before he goes after what's left of the cancer, unfettered in its ability to replicate inside your body. You try to reassure your rock, the man, who if he could, would reach inside you and take it for himself.

You realize that you no longer have any control over the parts of your life that cancer touches, which is just about all of it.

After surgery, you wait for the pathology report on the lymph node. With that behind you, you wait for the results of the bone scan. When you discover you might be one of the lucky ones, a wave of relief and gratitude washes over you.

Talking with amazing women at the cancer center who, despite battling horrific cancers, are radiant and supportive of each other, you understand that in those first few days and weeks, you are all alike. Everything but this falls away: you have cancer and you are scared.

Knowing that unlike many of them, your cancer should respond well to treatment, you begin to feel something else.

Why me?

The answer does not come.

You pray for the grace and inner strength of those who meet the challenge with such dignity. You pray they find healing, in whatever form it takes, and that they feel God's love cover them.

You see kindness everywhere: in those who are praying for you, those who show up at the hospital to support you, and in your sister- and brother-in-law who drive in from Dallas with plans for a fun-filled weekend to get your mind off things while you play the waiting game.

In their fear, everyone babys you. So you ask for special treats and privileges, just to give them something to do, reminding them, "I do have cancer, you know. I could die."

They catch on fast.

Irony is everywhere. A chest of drawers holds the three sexy new bras you bought two weeks before you were diagnosed. Now, you wonder if they make a 38C-32B.

You master new skills, like how to hold an IV pole with one hand while using the other to keep your hospital gown from going toilet surfing.

At work, where you've tried to keep it to yourself as you continue to do your job as you've always done, you wonder what your inquisitive co-workers think when they spot you in your editor's office behind closed doors. Most likely, that you've done something stupid and need a good talking to.

As for all those cell phone calls you've taken, walking outside to get some privacy, maybe they'll think you're having an affair.

Early on in this adventure, your husband gives you a greeting card depicting a lonely tent in the middle of a forest. Dozens of yellow eyes peer from the dark.

Inside are these words, good for all of us touched by cancer:

"Be brave, Little Camper."

Real man's throne guaranteed never to clog
Dec. 19, 2004

If a man's home is his castle, the toilet is the seat of power.

In our endless pursuit to make our almost-100-year-old home more comfortable, this summer Hubby decided to redo his bathroom. He wasn't crazy about the pink tile, worn-out floor and ugly cabinet.

And then there's the toilet.

My husband is 6-foot-5. The toilet rose about 18 inches above the floor, or at least that's the way it felt when he tried to fold his body into a seated position, knees practically at his chin. Both standing and sitting posed challenges; one called for skillful logistics coordination and the other produced arthritic knees.

For months, as I'd fall asleep at night, I'd hear the rustle of pages turning and an occasional, "Ooooh" and "Ummmm." You'd have thought it was the babes in the Sports Illustrated swimsuit issue, not the curves of a toilet bowl that captivated him.

I'd hear him mumbling in his sleep, "Right height. Right height."

He dragged me through every hardware store in town, stopping in front of the toilet displays.

"Look at this one," he said, pointing to a tall model. "Try it."

There are plenty of things I might want to do in a hardware store. Sitting on a toilet is not one of them.

He looked for weeks, until four little words on a display jumped out at him: "Guaranteed not to clog."

You'd have thought he'd won the lottery. For days after it was installed, I would find him standing in the bathroom doorway, staring at it.

If he'd installed it himself, I'd say he was doing what men are compelled to do: a little chest-beating as they admire their handiwork. But we'd called a plumber in for this bad boy. There was too much at stake.

A week or so after it was installed, my husband was giving friends a tour of the bathroom. With a sweep of the hand that would have done Vanna White proud, he pointed out the toilet.

"It's guaranteed not to clog," he said. "And it doesn't."

They looked at him. "Really. I tried it," he said.

"You what?" I asked.

He grinned.

"I tested it."

My husband is a practical sort. He'd thought about what an overflowing toilet would do to his newly remodeled bathroom, especially the travertine floor, new baseboard and pedestal sink and decided it would be a lot less stressful to find out in advance.

"What did you do?" I asked.

"Well," he said, "I put about a half a roll of toilet paper in it and then flushed it. It went, 'Whoosh!' and it was gone."

Pleased as could be, but not completely convinced, he put a whole roll in.

Hey, if it can flush a bowl full of golf balls, he figured, what's a few pounds of paper?

This toilet also uses less water. If you fully depress the lever, the oversized drain opens all the way and the water in the bowl just drops through. If you push it halfway down, water from the tank runs down the sides.

He pushed the lever. The gigantic blob of toilet paper started down, then with a sickening 'Glug,' closed off.

Figuring it needed more water, he pushed the lever halfway, then watched in horror as the bowl started filling. The water rose, higher and higher.

He was about to run for a plunger when the drain suddenly opened and "Whoosh!" it was gone.

Santa doesn't need to visit our home this year. We're flush.

Who knew that a hunk of porcelain in an 8-foot-by-8-foot patch of real estate could make a man so happy?

Moving past old wounds
March 20, 2005

I pulled into the driveway, turned off the engine and opened the car door. As I swung my legs out and prepared to stand, I heard the familiar clink of metal keys hitting concrete.

My left hand was full, so I stretched with my right, twisting to reach the wayward car keys.

Big mistake.

A sharp pain shot from my chest to my armpit, then raced up my arm. Everything burned.

It's been more than five months since a surgeon carved my breast open to get at the cancer living there.

In the process, he removed a significant portion of breast tissue and the sentinel lymph node, along with the cluster of cells eager to spread.

The breast healed well and radiation therapy went just fine, leaving me sore and streaked like a child's multi-hued art project.

When you first find out you have cancer, you are stunned by the force with which it consumes your life. It is as constant as the beating of your heart and the breath you take, an ever-present darkness that threatens to strip your life of joy. You think you'll never again wake up and wander through a day in blissful ignorance, with nothing more pressing than deciding whether to plant daffodils or daylilies.

It's the way of it, this sadness in looking back and seeing something clearly for the first time once it's irrevocably changed. You wonder if you'll ever again have an unaware moment.

And then you heal.

The thing about cancer, for me at least, is the completeness with which you forget it once owned you. I'm told there is no reason not to believe my cancer is gone. Done. I am cured. So I choose to believe that, and I go on.

When the soreness from the radiation faded and I again could move without feeling like there was not enough skin to stretch over my body, and when the scar on my breast began to fade, I began to think about the cancer less and less. It was as if it never happened.

And then I stretched to pick up a dropped set of keys.

Yes, my body still carries visible evidence of the cancer. I still have mirrors and my eyesight is fine. The little white pill I take every night is hard to ignore. But the rest of the time, nothing yells out, "Cancer! Cancer!"

You think you're healed. You think it's history, something that need never be revisited.

And then something pulls at the still-healing wound, and again, the source of the pain asserts its rights. See me. Feel me. Don't forget me.

Too often, the fear of what might happen if we let down our guard keeps us from moving past a wound and into healing. We have suffered, we tell ourselves, and remembering that will protect us in the future. It seems like a harmless enough delusion.

But it's awfully hard to awaken the joy that wasn't dead after all, merely slumbering, if we're too busy jealously guarding an old hurt.

Some wounds come from wood and metal. Others are wounds of the heart.

Both need tending.

Poppie gets it right

March 27, 2005

"Jarrod, let's move your glass back here while you're not drinking, OK?" I suggest to our youngest grandson during breakfast out Good Friday morning.

The glass, filled with very chocolately hot cocoa and topped with whipped cream, is perilously close to the edge of the table, considering Jarrod, like his Grammie, tends to talk with his hands.

One of the traditions we've established with "our boys" is to have breakfast at a restaurant near our house on Saturday morning after they've spent the night with us. This doesn't happen nearly as often as we'd like, but enough that they know what they can look forward to on those weekends.

We establish traditions in the hope that they will become lasting memories for the boys who too soon will become young men. We hope that the time spent with us will be memorable enough for them to include it on the list of things they loved growing up.

In our relationships with the boys, I'm the one who moves hot, sticky liquids out of harm's way while my husband finds any reason he can to say, "Yes," whatever the question might be.

While I'm busy trying to teach them why they shouldn't pick up coins from the floor in front of urinals in the bathroom and why booger fights at the table are not a good idea, their Poppie is busy teaching them how to belch in harmony.

He's awfully wise, our Poppie. While I'm offering lessons about life, he's far more interested in lessons of the heart.

Having married into our family when my daughter and son were well past the baby and toddler stage, he savors every moment with the boys, achingly aware of how quickly time will snatch those opportunities away.

Thursday night, while the boys lie curled together on the couch as they watch a movie, Poppie catches my attention and looks over at them, his face a study in pure, incurable love.

Store this picture in your memory bank, he telegraphs me, because there will come a day when brothers who can't bear to be out of touching range of each other will find the idea of any physical contact not associated with competition an intolerable thought.

After breakfast Friday morning, the boys get into Poppie's truck while I get into my car to drive to work.

"Grammie," Jordan calls to me through the open truck window, "I love you."

"I love you more," I tell him, an absolute truth.

I turn back to the car, only to hear him again, "Grammie."

"What, Baby," I ask.

He bends his chubby boy hand into the "come here" sign, curling his fingers in unison.

I walk to the truck, jealous that their Poppie will have all day to be with them, but happy that my three men will be making another memory.

Placing his chocolately hands on my face, Jordan leans in and gives me a big kiss, full on the lips, which is the way he thinks every kiss should be.

There are moments in our children's lives that we never forget. First word. First step. First day of school. The first time a son turns away in embarrassment from a goodbye kiss.

The blessing of this slippery kiss, the one my precious Jordan not merely tolerates but actually initiates, remains with me as I drive away from the restaurant.

In my rear view mirror, moving with a speed that takes my breath away, I watch his childhood disappear.

Off to the races

April 10, 2005

"My grandparents are vere special to me. They coock good food. They are vere specil to me."

That's the mini-essay our oldest grandson, Jordan, 7, wrote for his art project for "Grandparents Day" at his school recently.

I suspect the affectionate redundancy is less an exclamation mark than a convenient and hasty way to fill in that last empty line.

When Jordan tires of something, all he can think of is moving on to the next thing, post haste. I suspect this project was not his favorite task of the day.

"OK, children," I imagine his teacher telling the class, "write something about why your grandparents are special to you."

That gave Jordan the lead and the conclusion. All he had to add was a nut graph.

Beneath the essay were portraits of his Poppie and me, along with portraits of his Paw-Paw and Gigi.

He drew Poppie in a blue shirt and me in a red blouse. Astute choices, since blue is, indeed, Poppie's favorite color and I've been know to show up in red.

In his portrait, I have nice eyelashes and a big smile, but no nose. Poppie is noseless as well. I'm not quite sure what that means.

I do have nice, straight brown hair. Not exactly accurate, but then, the last time I checked, there wasn't a snow-white Crayon in the box.

Poppie showed up with black hair (he's blonde), so I guess black and brown complete Jordan's entire hair color repertoire.

Poppie and I look a little drab next to some of the other grandparents. Some grandmothers evidently have more good hair days than I do.

One in particular caught my eye, a really stylish woman, judging by the details drawn by her granddaughter, who has a career ahead of her as either a fashion designer or artist.

This Gram — I call her Gram because a woman like her would never allow herself to be called Grandmother — had saucy yellow curls, rosy cheeks, a striped blouse and, get this, earrings.

After checking out Jordan's work, I wandered down the hall to find our youngest grandson's art project for Grandparents Day.

"My grandparents and I like to go to my dad nacre rac," Jarrod, 6, wrote.

"Jarrod," I said to him later, surprised by this revelation. "I didn't know you had been to a NASCAR Race. Did one of your other grandparents take you?"

"No," he said cheerfully. "I just made it up."

While I'm not quite sure the assignment was meant to include fiction, it did get his imagination going, which needs very little help. This child can tell the best stories, delivered with gusto and rich with details.

What really got my attention was the accompanying drawing. It was a tableau of racecar heaven.

He drew three cars, red, blue and multicolored. I'm not sure about the last one, unless it's all that advertising. He even numbered them: 8, 18 and 11. I'll have to remember to ask him at some point how he chose the numbers. I'm sure there will be a story for that, too.

Across from the racetrack he drew a big patch of grass. Standing on it are three stick figures, which, I assume are his Dad and grandparents. I haven't asked which set yet, since I'd like to pretend it's us.

All in all, it's a pretty accurate rendering of an afternoon at the races, I'd say.

But then, I'm only guessing, having never been to a Nacre rac.

Fear can sneak up on you

May 1, 2005

"Janie, I'm sick."

The stroke, heart attack and heart surgeries that have irrevocably changed my mother's life the past few years also left their mark on her voice. What once was strong and sharp — as sharp and biting as her choice of words could be — has grown blurred around the edges.

But even with a bad cell phone connection, it was clear that her voice was weak and her words tinged with fear.

I'd called on a Sunday afternoon to check on her, thinking it would be a routine conversation. At least, as routine as this new relationship that we're forging across a half-century and two states will allow.

The three words made my heart lurch.

My mother is not one to throw weaknesses out there for just anyone to see, especially the daughter who shares more traits with her than she ever realized.

I, along with a sister and a niece, had been there to watch her surgery three years ago. We'd seen the bruised and failing veins pulse against her pale skin. We'd sat in an icy conference room as her doctor slashed thick lines across a pad to indicate how little blood could get through her battle-weary arteries.

We knew how fragile her heart, and her life, were.

The indignity of being dependent on others didn't rest well with a woman who'd worked hard all her life. A woman who could hold her own in any situation, or at least fake it, and who could wither with a single glance (another trait I seem to have inherited), was not pleased to have her vulnerability displayed.

"I'm all right" has become the mantra of her aging years. She says it often, delivering the hopeful lie much as she used to say, "I'll just take the wings."

At family get-togethers, we'd laugh about the way she could elevate martyrdom to a fine art.

This "I'm all right" is not a thinly veiled bid for attention. It's an attempt to reduce the worry she hears in my voice.

My mother has grown to believe that I love her.

Mother knows about worry. She knows about fixed incomes and the exorbitant cost of life-saving medications. She knows about bodies that betray us as they assert their right to go awry. She understands the futility of asking atrophied muscles and an impaired balance to propel her through everyday obstacles in a home where she is the only occupant.

When I told Mother about my breast cancer this past year, I waited on the end of a phone connection as tenuous as our relationship while she took it in. I imagined her face as she danced around the impossible idea of a mother outliving a child, an idea I quickly dispersed with the reassurance that this cancer was not a life-threatening one.

But security had been breached. Our conversations became a race to see who would be the first to say, "How are you feeling?"

It no longer was rhetorical.

So, on this Sunday afternoon, when she said, "Janie, I'm sick," I believed it.

We almost lost her. The last blood sugar reading before the ambulance arrived to take her to the hospital was five times the normal. She hadn't eaten in a couple of days, was dehydrated and confused.

She's home now, recuperating from pneumonia and adjusting to the idea of taking insulin. It's been a long battle, getting her to overcome the memory of being given too much insulin in the hospital during a previous stay, the one and only shot she allowed and quickly regretted.

Going into diabetic shock can put the fear of God into you.

The memory of the confusion, weakness, pain and fear that preceded this last trip to the hospital did what I couldn't. When Mother no longer could pretend that she could avoid insulin merely by eating almost nothing and simply willing her blood sugar to go down, she gave in.

I wish you could have heard the victory in her voice when she told me she'd taken her first shot at home.

"I'm not scared of it anymore," she said.

Conquering fear is no small matter. I'm paying close attention.

Two aunts, two different dispositions
July 10, 2005

A friend recently asked which adult I disliked most as a child —and why.

Because I tend to overanalyze just about everything, I'd usually have to ponder such a thing for a while.

Not with this question.

The name — and face — immediately came to mind.

My Aunt Helen was without a doubt one of the meanest women on earth. Frankly, she scared the beejebers out of me.

As a child, I instinctively knew that the woman who gave a brisk "Hello" and stuck out her bony arms for a hug was not a woman of warmth, compassion or authentic affection.

The greeting was for greeting's sake, not because she was happy to see you and couldn't wait to envelop you in her arms.

When my loving grandmother, who raised me, became sick, I was sent to live with Aunt Helen and Uncle T.J. a man who was as genial as she was cold.

For three years, I lived in an atmosphere of tension, criticism and unrealistic expectations, the exact opposite of everything I'd known the first seven years of life.

Every action was scrutinized and graded, every failure pointed out, accompanied by words like stupid and clumsy.

I learned that how I was valued and how I would be treated was entirely dependent on my meeting her expectations. She was constantly assessing my level of success (I can't remember but one, when she was satisfied with my grades) or failure (there were plenty of those to go around).

There were conditions to everything, especially approval.

And then there was my Aunt Bedie, who, being my grandmother's sister, actually was my great aunt.

Aunt Bedie was the adult I liked most as a child.

She was the sunniest, most loving and joyful human being I've ever known. I cannot recall ever seeing her angry or hearing her make a caustic or hateful remark.

I come from a big, close family that, when I was a child, sought any excuse to be together. Almost all of the family lived nearby and, when my grandmother was alive, gathered at her house for Sunday dinner.

In the summer, I'd spend a lot of time with aunts, uncles and cousins. Occasionally, I'd get to visit Aunt Bedie, which always made me happy.

She was a woman of endless patience who always made me feel loved. She'd spent hours playing games with me, bringing out her old dresses and heels so I could play dress-up.

She'd put a washtub full of water in the backyard to be warmed by the sun so I could take a bath, then wrap me in a sweet, line-dried towel.

"Smell this," she'd say with a big smile on laundry day, holding out sheets that she was folding. "Nothing else smells like sheets dried by a breeze in the sun."

At night, we'd lie in bed and talk. Sometimes she'd read to me from the Bible or her Watchtower. Although she wasn't a Jehovah's Witness, she greatly respected the fact that they took the time to visit her and leave her reading material.

From Aunt Helen, I got the dark drive for all things to be "right." All my adult life, I've battled her brainwashing that, when things don't go exactly as they "should" someone is at fault, and that person must be taken to task.

I didn't have someone to counteract her incessant criticism, to help me understand that things just happen, and that's OK.

So what if you drop something, or turn over a glass of milk, or God forbid, break something?

From my Aunt Bedie, I learned to find the joy in life, which is easy, because there are so many things to be grateful for.

I learned that I could be loved just because I, like all human beings, deserved it, not because I had made myself "perfect" enough to be loveable.

I learned to respect others, even those whose views differ from my own. I learned religious tolerance and to look for commonalties, not differences.

I learned to appreciate and savor life, though the dark side of me sometimes stretches out its own bony fingers and threatens to snatch that joy and peace away.

And I learned that love is a visible, touchable, tangible commodity that cannot be faked.

Grandchildren bring that lesson home in a very personal way. With grandchildren, you get a second chance.

"Our job," my very wise husband once told me, remembering his own mean aunt, "is to love our boys. Nothing else. Just love them, so that their memories of us are good ones."

So I breathe a little prayer, with equal measures of gratitude and

trepidation: "Please, God, give me what it takes to be an Aunt Bedie."
Amen.

Grandson puts his fears aside, worries about others
August 7, 2005

The chatter of proud parents, grandparents, aunts and uncles as they spilled through the auditorium doors quickly turned to "ooohs" as they saw the lightning bolts and heard the thunder roll across darkening skies.

The after-summer wrap-up program for the youngsters was a gas. Few things are more fun than watching a bunch of hyped-up kids singing their hearts out and bouncing around on stage with equal parts of shyness and abandon.

Our oldest grandson, Jordan, who was spending the night with us, had been making the rounds of the parking lot, saying hello to friends and their parents when he heard the first big boom and saw lightning split the clouds.

He stopped, ducked slightly and headed for Poppie, who was his ride, since we were in two cars.

I gave him a hug and told him I'd see him at home.

They had a five-minute head start and I fell behind in heavy traffic that slowed for the downpour. About 10 minutes into the 30-minute drive, my cell phone rang.

"Grammie," Jordan said, in that serious little man voice he so often uses, "Where are you? I can't see you."

"I'm about 10 minutes behind you, Baby," I said.

"Poppie," he said to my husband, "Can we wait for Grammie?"

"Sure, Buddy," Poppie said, touched by his concern. "Tell her we'll wait at the bank parking lot."

Five minutes later, the cell phone went off again.

Jordan, whose boredom threshold can be low, had been watching for me. He asked his Poppie, "How long have we been waiting?" Poppie told him about five minutes. "How long will it take before she gets here?"

For a 7-year-old, even concern carries an expiration date.

About that time Jordan spotted headlights and told Poppie, "I bet that's Grammie."

When the car passed, he said sadly, "No, that's not her."

"Poppie," Jordan said a minute later, "Can I call Grammie?

"Grammie" he said, when I answered, "I think Annie needs us. We need to go home now."

"I think that's a good idea," I told him, releasing him from Grammie-watching duty and toward some family pet time. "I know Annie can't wait to see you."

When he hung up, Jordan turned to Poppie and said, "Grammie will be OK."

In a couple of minutes, Jordan, looking at the sky, said, "Poppie, can I use your phone again? I need to call Mom and make sure she's OK."

He dialed his home number. It rang several times.

"She's not there, Poppie. We need to go check on her."

Finally the machine came on. "Mom, WHERE ARE YOU? This is Jordan. I'm worried about you."

When Mom finally picked up, his voice brightened considerably. "Mom, is that you? I was worried. Are you OK?"

When they finished talking, he asked to speak to his little brother, who had stayed home with Mom.

"Hi, Jarrod. It's Jordan. Are you OK?"

When the storm first started, before Jordan made his first call to me, he'd been fixated on the weather, asking Poppie, "Are those bad storms out there? Can the lightning get us in the car?"

No, Poppie reassured him, the inside of the car was a very safe place.

As grandparents, we pray that every place will provide safe shelter for a child who puts aside his own fears to make sure the people he loves most are safe. It's an awfully big responsibility for such a little boy.

In the assurance of our safety, he finds his own.

$\mathcal{S}ection \; \mathcal{S}even$

October 9, 2005 to January 28, 2007

FROM LEFT, DENIS AND JOEL;
SHERRY AND BRENDA MCBRIDE

Hurricanes and house guests

Oct. 9, 2005

Stick three road-weary and hurricane-stressed adults, two boisterous boys, a dog and a turtle into a home with four adults, two cats and a dog of its own and you'll quickly find out what manner of mettle you possess.

I am not the woman I thought I was.

Day One: Fifteen hours after we loaded down two vehicles with 5/6 of our nuclear family for what usually is a five-hour drive, we unloaded hundreds of pounds of evacuee flotsam and jetsam into my sister- and-brother-in-law's Dallas home.

They greet us with warm hugs. Stay as long as you like, they say. You're family.

Annie, our affable mutt, comes nose-to-nose with Rocky, a Rottweiler and German shepherd mix who lives to guard. We pull them apart. It's obvious that we will have to stagger potty breaks for the dogs.

We plop ourselves in front of the TV and watch Rita, terrified for the family and friends who stayed behind and wondering if we still have homes.

Day Two: They're treating us like guests. They won't let us buy any groceries nor do any housework. This is not acceptable for those of us with an aversion to not pulling our own weight.

I am smitten with Anderson Cooper and his cool demeanor. I also am depressed, disconnected from everything I know, including the people at work who stayed behind to do the work I want to be doing. I look at my grandbabies and my daughter, who is a single parent, and try to tell myself I made the right decision in leaving.

Day Four or Five: I finally connect with one of my co-workers and discover five of us have set up a temporary bureau at the Dallas Morning News. The depression lifts; I have a purpose again.

My brother-in-law, who loves us and would do almost anything for us, becomes snippier by the minute. I cannot blame him. I set a goal of becoming invisible.

Day Who Cares: How to keep the peace: don't stack the bowls from right to left in the dishwasher. Don't hang the dishrag over the sink. Don't open the refrigerator so much. Pick up the dog's poop with a shovel and toss it over the back fence (and if you're too short, watch it come tumbling back down your arm).

Day "When can I go home?": I hate my brother-in-law. He hates me. I hate their dog and their schizophrenic cat and I want to throw the television remote control in the drainage ditch.

I no longer am a patient, thoughtful guest. I am pouty, overwrought and mad as hell. I curl into a ball and weep for hours.

My brother-in-law greets us every morning with "Do you have power back yet?"

It gets worse before it gets better. But it does get better.

I don't hate my brother-in-law. He doesn't hate me. We both, however, are in no hurry to be roomies again any time soon.

I decide the first thing I'm going to do when I get home is run through the house naked. I'm going to squeeze toothpaste from the middle and fold towels any damned way I please.

There are many, many lessons in this hurricane experience. Here's one:

Love will get you through almost anything, but you might look a little different when you come out the other side.

Never first

Oct. 30, 2005

Living in the country carries a price tag.

We live 30 minutes from our grandbabies, which might not seem like much, but it's a far cry from living down the street.

I'd love for the boys to be able to pick up the phone and say, "Grammie, come see what I made" and five minutes later, I'm at the door. I'd love to stop on the way home and drop off a treat or go over their homework. But work, their home and our home are 30 minutes apart, each a different way, which tends to kill spontaneity, though we don't let it slow us down much.

Which bring us to Halloween.

"You realize, don't you," my husband said the other night, "that our boys will never come here to trick or treat."

"Never," he repeated.

"I know," I told him, "but we can see them in their costumes."

We know that asking the boys' mom to come by our house would be not only unreasonable, but selfish. Why should the boys spend an hour in a car on a night that's all about walking the neighborhood, going from house to house?

Jarrod, the younger of the two, spent this past Sunday with us.

Our church has a pumpkin patch, and Hubby was signed up to work. The boys walked around and Jordan, being older, got to pick out the pumpkin.

Jarrod, whose fate is forever sealed as the youngest, asked if he could stay with us when his mom and Jordan went home.

The minute she left, Jarrod went on a 45 minute search for The Perfect Pumpkin, after I'd suggested he pick one out so we could carve a jack o' lantern.

He finally settled on a plump, tall one and we took it home to work magic. We Googled pumpkins and he chose a face with witches' caps for eyes, a ghost for the nose and a Batman mouth.

Oooooooooh.

I cut the top off, gave Jarrod some rubber gloves and we started scooping out the goop.

"Can we eat the seeds?" he asked.

"You bet," I told him. "We'll toast them later."

We never made it that far. It took an hour to get it clean, between talking about everything from the moon to hurricanes. Front porch conversations with a child are the best kind.

Once it was ready to carve, we loaded it up and took it to the pumpkin patch so Poppie wouldn't have to miss out.

We took lots of photos, including a posed one of Jarrod holding the knife as if he were carving, just to give his mom a heart attack. It was, of course, Poppie's suggestion.

When we took The Perfect Pumpkin home, he raced inside. "Mom," he asked, face shining, "Do you LOVE my pumpkin?"

"Yes, Jarrod," she said. "I LOVE your pumpkin. It's the best pumpkin I've ever seen."

It was the perfect thing to say to a boy who cannot escape being born second, a boy forever destined to find a way to carve out his own spot.

25 year adventure

Dec.18, 2005

"A smart woman knows her limitations and asks for help. That's something you need to learn."

It wasn't exactly what I wanted to hear when I asked my husband to open a cantankerous pull-top can of fruit.

I gave him the look. The one he says I perfected early in our marriage.

"Well, Dear," he said. "It's true. That's not a bad thing. We all have limitations."

My husband and I celebrated our 25th wedding anniversary this past week. Living with the same person for 25 years will teach you a lot, not only about your mate, but about yourself.

The fierce independence I brought to our marriage caused conflict countless times during the first few years. While I don't like being dependent on anyone, my husband views his primary job as a husband to take care of things.

In his eyes, my dependence on him means he's doing things right.

Independence in a relationship isn't the only issue on which my husband and I have differed.

We both have strong opinions on most everything, from which way the toilet paper unrolls to carpet versus wood floors.

Friday morning, as we sat and talked about how much we enjoyed our date out to celebrate our anniversary, I asked, "So what else have you learned about me during the past 25 years?"

He laughed, then rattled off a list.

"Don't talk to you in the morning. Don't do anything without permission — and then get the permission in writing. If I tell you something, I need proof. Otherwise, you won't believe it, unless you read it somewhere or a stranger told you."

I gave him the look. He just laughed.

"We can't agree on anything," he said. "When we buy a car, we can't agree on the color. We can't agree on decorating styles. We can't agree on movies. Just going out to eat is a challenge. Our communication styles are different. In our marriage, it's been a long list of who, what, when and where discussions.

"But that's O.K.," he said. "Marriage is an adventure. And it should be. Marriage shouldn't be placid.

"I've learned to let you win," he continued. "Give in and give up. That's my motto. Roll over and play dead and life is much easier."

Those who know my husband are laughing as they read this. He has a very strong will and isn't afraid to express his thoughts.

But there is no question he considers me in every decision he makes, and that he cares deeply about my happiness.

He's held my hand and held me up through many challenges, including breast cancer.

He is my heart, my soul, my life, and if God gives us another 25 years together, then that's just fine with me. I could use a new adventure or two — within reason, of course.

Despite the reminders, hope remains
Jan. 22, 2006

I hardly think about the cancer anymore.

It isn't because there are no reminders; they are everywhere. Pink ribbons, e-mails from friends asking for prayers for the newly diagnosed, a soapy hand sliding across the hollow where a breast once curved.

Somewhere along the way, cancer becomes the thing that happened.

Past tense.

Mismatched breasts become the norm, as familiar as the ridge of an old knee wound.

I am reminded of this as I read the cancer journal I started shortly after being diagnosed but eventually abandoned, at risk of letting it consume every thought.

It brings it back, like a bruise no longer visible but still tender to touch.

I remember the hard body shell that held me in place during radiation treatments, molded to keep me immobile so the killing rays are contained to the tumor as much as possible, though countless healthy cells become collateral damage.

At the end of treatment, I watch the radiation therapist hang it near a dozen more, stark white sarcophaguses now empty and spent, rattling when disturbed.

"I guess you throw those away," I remark, knowing they fit one body, and one alone, but also imagining mine cast out, the way I hope the cancer has been.

No, they tell me, they'll deflate them, clean them and mold them to a new patient.

I stare at the line of molds, wondering about the women whose bodies have been restrained in them before mine. How did they handle the fear? Did they pray? Curse God? Or maybe broker a deal?

Later, after I dress, I walk to the clothes hamper and stand there, fingering the hospital gown I'd worn almost daily for six weeks. The technician, taking note of my hesitation, asks if I want to take it home.

Briefly, I consider it, remembering the worn, soft cotton blanket I took home from M.D. Anderson after my surgery, the one that warmed me while I waited to be taken to the operating room and which my husband gently wrapped around me with trembling fingers as he stood over my bed waiting for me to awaken.

It has become the Blankie I never had. On days when I am troubled by some worry, hurt or disappointment, I reach for it. When my daughter, exhausted from being a single mom and career woman, lies on my couch on a lazy Sunday afternoon, I cover her with it.

No, I tell the technician, but thanks for the offer.

I hold the gown with both hands and close my eyes, trying to visualize the next woman who will pull it over her vulnerable body.

I whisper a prayer that she finds comfort, strength, faith and healing. And then I send the gown on its way.

My breast always will have the memory of the radiation burn. I cannot expose it to sunlight without protection. When I take a warm shower, the triangular outline again becomes visible. No creams, no potions, no matter how often applied, will heal it completely.

In the journal, I write, "Will I be like that? Will I remain unhealed, marked for the rest of my life?"

It's still early, but I am hopeful.

Tell me about that girl in the photo
March 12, 2006

I think I would have liked her.

The girl smiling from a silver frame atop the bookcase is impossible to miss. No matter how many times I walk by, if my eyes turn in that direction, they fall on her.

She's a slip of a girl, thick dark hair pulled back, rebellious waves anchored with bobby pins.

Dark lipstick, a bright crimson, perhaps, frames a heartbreakingly eager smile.

Her pale dress, cinched at the waist and gathered beneath the bust, shows a fine figure, not too skinny, curved where a woman-in-the-making should be.

She stands with hands on hips, back arched, one heel raised in the 1940s glamour girl pose that graced the movie screens and gossip magazines of the day.

The woman in the picture, my mother at 17, is alive with possibility.

When my mother married for the second time, she and her new husband moved to the other end of the earth — Texas — leaving me, less than a year old, to be raised by her parents in Arkansas.

I saw Mother only a few days a year, if that much. By the time I had the opportunity to store memories, they were of a woman whose body had carried eight children, endured a back-breaking waitress job, and faced the mind-numbing reality that things quite likely wouldn't change.

It's not as if she hadn't felt the sharp edges of life. As a girl, she worked in the fields without complaining, helping to tend the youngest of her seven sisters and brothers and doing more than her share of chores, my aunts tell me.

Marriage was defined by the social structure of rural life of the day. That, and her parent's reality: a cold, oppressive man whose wants and needs always came first, and a warm, strong woman who found solace in her children and her garden.

But when you're young, the mind has a way of pushing what is into a back corner, replacing it with what might be. When she dreamed of what might be, what did she see? As the first in her family to graduate from high school, did she long to move to the city and build a career? Or was the fantasy of being some handsome, gentle man's cherished wife as far as she would allow herself to see?

The woman in the picture isn't saying. That's the thing about photographs. They let you in only so far.

My mother's and my relationship is tenuous. It hasn't come easily and remains a fragile thing. During the last couple of years, during brief visits and weekly phone conversations, she's allowed an occasional glimpse of who she was, and is.

Then, just as quickly, she closes the door.

The next time I see her, I'm going to take that photograph with me. Tell me about this girl, I'll say.

Likely, she'll laugh and make some sarcastic remark that does exactly what she intends it to, deflect closer scrutiny.

I'm not giving up that easily.

Only my mother knows the girl captured in that sepia image. It's time I got to know her, as well.

Perhaps we can take a new photo, one that my daughter someday will pass by, pausing to wonder about the two women whose smile she shares.

Find peace in the imperfection of your father
June 18, 2006

The process of living provides an ever-changing source of hurts.

In writer Sherman Alexie's wonderful 1998 film, "Smoke Signals," one of the central characters, Victor, feels compelled to retrieve his estranged father's ashes when he hears of his death. When the alcoholic father who made Victor's life miserable with his presence deserted his family, he complicated it by his absence.

Victor's wound, 20 years old, still is raw. He hated his father for living, and now, he hates him for dying.

By film's end, Victor comes to understand that his father, and his story, are more complicated than the wounded child knew.

The simplicity with which a child views his or her world is absolute. Pain hurts. Someone is at fault.

But our relationships with our fathers seldom are simple. For those of us whose fathers were not present, life is a long journey in search of him.

Because I didn't know who my father was until I was in my 40s, I had no long list of transgressions to pore over. There was only one: his absence.

For those whose ever-present fathers were a source of fear or pain, the list grew in direct proportion to memory.

During the end credits of Smoke Signals, a voiceover reads Dick Lourie's poem, "Forgiving Our Fathers," which captures the absurdly endless possibility for failure:

". . . maybe for leaving us too often or forever when we were little/ maybe for scaring us with unexpected rage or making us nervous because there seemed never to be any rage there at all/for marrying or not marrying our mothers, for divorcing or not divorcing our mothers . . ."

If we forgive our fathers, the poet asks, what is left?

Before we can fill that place where resentment once lived, we have to explore another question: what will it take — and, perhaps, cost — us to forgive?

Our fathers, like Victor's, are complicated individuals who exist outside of their role as Dad. Like each of us, they are capable of great successes and abysmal failures. The live, breathe, work and worry. They carry enormous stress. Some handle it with a certain amount of grace. Others are crushed by it.

Some had good examples to follow. Others had dismal role models, if any.

Fathers who wounded us with their emotional absence or cowed us with their rage, who made us fear failure or seek its safety, who loved us too little or too much, failed to nurture us as we deserved.

Without dismissing our right to protect and nurture ourselves, we only can hope to find some understanding of our fathers independent of ourselves.

I loved my father from the moment I met him. In the five years we had before he died, the joy he took in getting to know me and the unconditional love he offered filled an emptiness nothing else had been able to do. Dismissing him because I believed that he had dismissed me would have robbed me of that blessing, and the sense of completeness it brought.

Forgiveness, as complicated as the source of the transgressions that call for it, is a singularly personal process.

I wouldn't presume to suggest that anyone else's situation mirrors my own, or that forgiveness is the answer.

My prayer is that each of you finds your own peace, in your own way.

A friend in need is ripe for ridicule
Aug. 13, 2006

"Hi, Brenda. Is Jerry home?" my husband asked on the phone.
"Yes. Why?"
The "why" is typical Brenda. As a kindergarten teacher, she asks questions all day, stimulating her kids' minds and developing their curiosity, which is one of the reasons she's so good at what she does.

Instead of saying, "Sure" and handing Jerry the phone, she wants details.

We love her for it.

"Because," my husband, the caller said, "I need him to come get me off the roof."

"Why can't you get off the roof?"

"Because I'm stupid," he said cheerfully. "I can't reach the ladder."

"We'll be right there."

Brenda and Jerry live down the street. They are the kind of neighbors you can count on, even when you do something goofy. Yes, there will be unmerciful teasing involved, but hey, we can live with that, since no one is better at dishing it out than my husband.

They are the kind of people who deliver pine straw to us so we can mulch the flowerbeds. Brenda will drop by for a glass of wine and leave a lovely silver-topped bottle stopper behind.

Like our other great neighbors, Travis and Jan, who brought the whole family over to cut tree limbs and haul them off when Hurricane Rita hit us hard, Brenda and Jerry are as generous as they come.

So, you might ask, how did he get stranded?

A recent storm knocked a major limb from the huge oak tree in our back yard. It didn't fall all the way, getting hung up on a big knot. Getting it down safely offered many challenges.

So, of course, my husband decides to do it while he is alone. He does this intentionally, knowing that I'd prefer to be there. Not because I can offer any real help or stop him from doing something foolhardy, which I can't, but I can at least dial 911 as he lies there maimed and bleeding.

He formulated his plan of attack. He'd get on the roof and tie a rope around the limb so he could pull it away from the house from a safe distance.

Instead of getting the extension ladder, which would have required walking a few more yards to the storeroom, he grabbed a nearby stepladder.

He had to get on the very top rung to crawl on the roof. You'd think he'd realize that this was not an ideal situation.

Nope.

So there he is, ready to dismount. But the ladder is waaaay down there, below a slick roof, which he discovers as he loses control and slides right to the edge.

I pick just that moment to call him from work. Luckily, he has his cell phone in his pocket.

"Hey, Sweetie," I say. "I have to work late tonight."

"OK," he says.

That's it. He's stuck on a roof and all he says is, "OK."

So he hangs up and calls Jerry.

Which, of course, Jerry loves. He drives down with Brenda, steps out of the car, opens the gate and stands there, grinning.

"Have you got your checkbook handy?" he asks.

Brenda, brow wrinkled, looks up, tilts her head and says, "So why are you on the roof?"

Get help – and get the man in your life to a prostate exam

Sept. 10, 2006

"How do I love thee? Let me count the ways . . ." begins Elizabeth Barrett Browning's Sonnet No. 43 from the Portuguese.

I'm thinking of writing a slightly less adoring one that begins, "How do I get thee to the doctor for a checkup? Let me count the ways . . ."

September is National Prostate Cancer Awareness Month, a fact my husband is determined to ignore.

It's been six years (six!) since he has had a complete physical exam.

Six. Years.

I am as faithful as they come about making and keeping regularly scheduled checkups.

Breast cancer will do that for you.

Even before the cancer, for a number of years I scheduled my yearly gynecological exam and mammogram on my birthday, a gift to those I love and don't want to leave without a wife, mother, grandmother or friend.

Statistics say most of us will encounter a serious health issue at some point. My husband acts as if he's immune to that.

What is it about men that makes them so reluctant to see a doctor? Years of commiserating with fellow wives has taught me that this is a trait men cling to with the stubbornness of a donkey, or as they call them in the animal world, jackass.

"Who, me?" they say when called on it.

My husband is an intelligent, professional 50-year-old who makes misbehaving computers tremble at the sight of him, yet he shies away from a doctor's office. It isn't that he's afraid. He's not. He knows that a checkup, including a digital rectal exam, is not painful. He just does not like the process of making an appointment, keeping it, sitting in a waiting room and then undressing for a relative stranger. Go figure.

When I push him on making an appointment, he says, "I don't have time."

Yes, he works long hours and is spread awfully thin, but now, really. I know they can spare him for a few hours.

When I offer to place the call and make the appointment, he says, "I don't know if I'll be able to get away then."

It doesn't matter when "then" is. In his dream world, you call a doctor up and say, "My schedule just cleared up. I'll be there in 15 minutes."

The concept of making an appointment weeks ahead makes him crazy. Join the club, I tell him. Besides, as we women know, it's just an excuse.

So, here's the plan. I'm enlisting the help of all of you out there who are recipients of my husband's computer expertise and have become friends as a result.

When he drops by your offices to whip your errant servers into shape, ask him, "So, have you made that prostate screening appointment yet?"

I'm hoping a few dozen blushes later, he'll reconsider.

Feel free to do the same thing for the man in your life.

Holding on – and leaving behind
Dec. 17, 2006

Wednesday, my husband and I celebrated 26 years of marriage.

I learned a long time ago that pride is best kept under control, lest one invite the fall that is sure to come, so don't expect any bragging about my role in our success story.

It would be rather duplicitous, in any case, since the credit goes to the Big Guy — who made an instant impression on me with his huge heart, unbridled sense of enthusiasm, unabashed sentimental nature, disarming honesty, sharp mind, goofy wit and fierce loyalty.

I will, however, share what I have learned during those years.

The syncretism in our relationship cannot be ignored; the yin and yang of our personalities have caused as much consternation as they have breathed life into our family.

While we share core beliefs, we approach life differently, whether it's finances, furnishings or failure.

My husband is a risible sort, with a sense of humor that is absolutely untamable, much as I have, on occasion, tried to subdue it in the interest in decorum.

I am easily embarrassed; he laughs — especially at himself — louder than anyone in the room.

To his credit, he usually ignores my caution and continues to make everyone around him laugh. Few people can lighten a mood the way he can.

On the importance of being oneself, he is unyielding. It is tantamount to dishonoring the gifts we are given, he believes, and he has, not without resistance, made a believer of me, though I still encourage him to consider refining those gifts now and then.

When Hurricane Rita's anniversary came around a few months ago, I found myself reflecting on the lessons it brought. When it threatened our home, we spent a lot of time deciding what to take with us and what to leave behind.

How wise we would be to put that much thought into doing the same thing when we join ourselves to another as a life partner.

In marriage, we bring the better parts of ourselves into the union. Unfortunately, we also tend to drag along old wounds, bad habits, and an inflexibility that is counter-productive. We guard these abysmally bad friends as if they were treasures, though we would be better served to let the hurricane blow them away.

While Rita produced stress, and plenty of it, it reminded us of the power of solidarity. In a crisis, it is us against them, whether the "them" is cancer, a hurricane or a bitter disappointment.

The "us" is the sum total of our commitment, love and shared experiences. It is our family unit, the unquestionable core of which is my husband.

The morning of our anniversary, I was sitting at the computer in our home office and had a question. Without pausing to turn around, I called out, "Where are you?"

"Right here," he said from behind me, with that warm, sensuous voice that stopped my heart the first time I heard it, "where I always have been, and always will be."

I've never believed anything more.

The gift of confidence
Dec. 24, 2006

It's almost Christmas and the house is a wreck. Toys, crumpled clothes, scuffed shoes and gum wrappers litter the floor.

Follow that trail, guided by electronic beeps, and you'll end up in front of two boys high on sugar and the thought of a big pile of presents headed their way.

We live for moments like this.

On the nights we have them for a sleepover, at bedtime, I always make several stops in our grandsons' room. The first is to tell them goodnight. The second is to remind them it's time to go to sleep. The third is reminder number two. The fourth is to stare at their sweet faces relaxed in slumber.

By trip number three, 7-year-old Jarrod is lost in the sleep of the satisfied. Jordan, 9, tends to lie awake for a while, his mind going places we can only guess at before finally succumbing to sleep.

As I look at him, it strikes me that, while the little boy he once was still resides within, Jordan is becoming an adolescent.

I wish we could hold him here a little longer.

Jordan is our intense, inward-looking, deep-thinking child. You have to follow his lead, interpreting whether the signals he send say "My space, do not enter" or "You can come in now, but only as long as I say so."

I lean close — so that this child who is so hard on himself can see my face — and tell him, "Jordan, I am absolutely crazy about you."

"What's making you crazy?" he asks, puzzled by the phrase.

I laugh and tell him again, "I'm crazy about you. You are just the neatest kid ever."

His eyes lock on mine and he smiles. I kiss him goodnight and turn to leave.

"Grammie," he says, with the slightest of hesitation.

"What, Baby."

"What's neat about me?"

I hold my breath.

When a child like Jordan issues this kind of invitation, you snatch it before he can change his mind. While he is known to find ways to stall bedtime, my grandmother's heart intuits that, tonight, this is not the case.

"Well, Buddy," I say, "just about everything."

I sit on the edge of the bed and go down the list, trying to think of what insecurities nudge him. Choosing my phrases carefully, I tell him how smart he is, what a big, generous heart he has, how observant he is and how much he sees that others miss. How funny he is when he mangles jokes and what a good big brother he is.

While I'm telling him these things, I feel his fingers on my arm, as light as the brush of an angel's wing. I gratefully file this feeling away, aware of how fleeting such moments are.

The Christmas gift I would give Jordan this year, if I could, is an unshakeable belief in himself, a sense of how valued, and worthy of love he is.

I am comforted knowing that he is well on his way to finding that, being blessed with a devoted, insightful mother who is so in tune with her sons that no matter where she is, at any given moment, she can close her eyes and hear the rhythm of their hearts, beating in tandem with her own.

It is our job to augment that, and to make sure that the last thoughts these amazing children have as they drift off to sleep are ones of contentment and peace.

May yours be, as well.

Men's weekly luncheon provides therapy
Jan. 28, 2007

"Now see," my husband said, shaking his head, "this is exactly why I need my Friday therapy lunch."

"What do you mean?"

"Because at least I know I'm not the only one with a wife who can't make decisions but who wants to be in control."

Oooooh.

My husband, frustrated by the time I was taking choosing flooring for our kitchen, was talking about a group of five guys he lunches with regularly. And here I thought that — unlike the women on ABC TV's "The View" who gossip and dish dirt — these guys were sitting around talking about football and cars and hot wings.

"So," I said, "you guys talk about your wives at lunch?" knowing he loves to chat with clients about whatever is going on in his life at the moment — and heaven knows I give him so much to work with.

While the women in their lives are by no means the primary topic at lunch, he assured me, they have at times "compared notes," hoping to get "at least some glimpse into how women think."

"So," I said, "what have you learned during these conversations about the differences between men and women?"

The words had barely left my mouth before he ticked them off: "We don't think alike. We don't act alike. We don't have the same sense of humor. When we tell a joke we like to our wives, they don't think it's funny."

Knowing the lame jokes he's brought home from those lunches, I can imagine the other women's responses. Clever, witty, subtle, these jokes are not.

What else, I asked?

"Well," he said, "they all think it's hilarious that I actually voice my opinion to you."

"What do you mean?" I asked.

My husband explained it's like the wise, silent one of the guys who listens much more than he speaks once told him: "Joel, you just don't get it. When a woman asks a question, she's not really asking your opinion. She's just thinking out loud."

"And . . ." I said.

"They're trying to convince me I need to know when to shut up," he said.

My husband said, one of the guys once told him: "When most people find themselves digging a hole, they put the shovel down. Not you. You get a stick of dynamite and see how big you can make the hole."

About a year ago, when I asked to join in on the lunch fun, the guys decided to open it to the women for one week only. They planned lunch at a local cafeteria.

"Let's pick a different place," I suggested. "That's a big open room with mass tables and no privacy and it's not comfortable or conducive to conversation."

Hubby took it to the guys.

"Now see," the head guy who organizes the lunches said, "That's exactly why women can't come. They just try to take over."

They withdrew the invitation.

Note to guys: Valentine's Day is right around the corner ... and we know some great restaurants that have wonderful ambience and are conducive to conversation and . . . well, just say the word.

Section Eight

May 6, 2007 to May 10, 2009

LISA RENEE LIGDA BEAULIEU

Community's kindness
helps family deal with loss

May 6, 2007

You think you know a thing or two about kindness and the human heart and then God gives you a good thump on the head and says, "Pay attention here. This is important."

And, him being God and all, you listen.

During this past week, as our family has grieved over the loss of Beaumont Police Officer Lisa Renee Ligda Beaulieu, we have been the recipients of numerous acts of kindness.

Lisa was our daughter, sister, granddaughter, niece, aunt, cousin and friend, but you've let us know that you considered her a member of your family, too.

During these difficult days, we have been reminded a thousand times that we are not alone in our grief, as those who worked with Lisa, knew her or simply respected the profession she chose, closed rank to protect us.

In their grief, they did the only thing they could: attend to those whom Lisa loved, and who loved her. They committed to being there for Lisa and her family until Lisa was laid to rest, and nothing could have kept them away.

They were there when it was hard to be: on the accident scene and at the hospital as emergency personnel and doctors did everything they could to save her.

They escorted her to the morgue and stood guard there, as they did around the clock at the funeral home.

At every step, they conducted themselves with dignity and professionalism.

Lisa loved being a cop. She had to overcome a number of obstacles to earn her badge, and I wish you could have seen her face at the swearing in ceremony when she wore it for the first time.

Lisa's footprints are all over this community. Every day, she interacted with its citizens and learned how to conduct herself as its representative. Lisa understood that she was part of something bigger than herself, and she wanted to rise to the challenge.

For the last week, we have done our best to represent her well. As her mother, my sister Gloria, said, Lisa would expect no less.

We've heard dozens of Lisa stories, things only those on the receiving end would know. Every act of kindness, every moment of generosity Lisa extended has come home to us a thousand fold.

Here are just a few that brought us comfort:

* Officers standing formal honor guard over Lisa's coffin.
* A constant line of people during visitation offering their condolences, cards from coworkers and the touch of a boss' hand on a shoulder.
* Delicate pink ribbons fluttering from the radio antennas of motorcycles that escorted the family to the funeral and to the cemetery.
* Children from a local middle school anti-drug program who staked out a spot near the front entryway of the Beaumont Civic Center so we wouldn't miss their hand-lettered sign.
* A bouquet of flowers on the hood of Lisa's car.
* A man holding a sign, "Thank you, Lisa."
* The line of cadets standing in formation in front of Lamar Institute of Technology, holding a flag and saluting Lisa as the hearse

and family cars rolled by.

* The sea of officers standing in the heat at the civic center and later, at the cemetery.

* Vietnam veterans, industrial workers in coveralls and office workers in suits and heels, lining the funeral route.

Each of you brought us comfort and we will forever be grateful to those who took time from their lives to honor the loss of hers.

Tending to Mom's repaired heart
June 3, 2007

For 18 years now, I've never gone longer than 10 days without writing. The insistent procession of words in my head and the rhythm of my hands against a keyboard have become as much a part of my life as sleeping and waking.

But, for the past 16 days, the journalist in me has been replaced by the child as I keep watch over my ailing mother in an Arkansas hospital.

At 80, my mother's health already was fragile. After a quadruple bypass seven years ago, two stents, a stroke, uncontrolled diabetes and other issues, her quality of life had deteriorated to the point that she was forced to make a difficult decision. The only thing that could help, doctors explained, was to replace her aortic valve, a long and arduous surgery for a woman her age.

While the surgery held inherent risks, Mother felt she couldn't continue to live as she has for some time, so weak and out of breath that she couldn't walk across a room.

She put her affairs in order, made her peace with God and told us, blue eyes fixed on ours to make sure we understood, that she was ready for whatever happened.

Some time ago, I promised Mother that if she had another heart surgery, I would be there for it, as I had been the first time.

So, when the surgery was scheduled, I requested vacation time and headed to Arkansas.

Our relationship has always been a complicated one. During childhood, I never lived with my mother, but her absence held sway over my life with a power I've never fully understood.

Through the years, we've worked on our relationship. While I knew, and accepted, that most of that would fall to me, Mother eventually began to respond and did her best to meet me along the way as we tried to move from the past into the kind of future we hoped to share.

It hasn't been easy. My mother is a complicated, intense, prickly woman, who doesn't give of herself easily. Her wounds have made her wary, distrustful and combative. She is as quick to anger as she is to hurt.

I carry my own wounds, as we all do, but I learned long ago that we have a choice. We can continue to pick at the scabs, or let them heal.

I choose healing.

Somewhere along this uneven path, so gradually that I can't say when, my mother began to offer up bits of faith, trust and even affection. She let me in, little by little, reminding me once in a while that it all could disappear within seconds if I did something to displease her.

So, along with my baby sister, Susan, my Aunt Shirley and Aunt Gladys, Cousin Wanda and my husband, I sat in a family room during the eight-hour surgery, while my other siblings who couldn't be there waited for news.

We rejoiced when her surgeon said it had gone well. Then, two hours later, despaired when bleeding forced him to go in again for another two hours of surgery.

The last two weeks, I've watched Mother struggle to stay alive long enough for her exhausted kidneys and fragile lungs to begin to heal.

She is unable to speak because of the respirator we hope will allow her lungs to strengthen. Because of that, all I can do is look into those fear-filled and anxious blue eyes, offer whatever comfort I can, and advocate for her the best I can. Susan has now joined me in these efforts and her presence has been a blessing to Mother, and to me.

Each day, hour and minute, we are alternately encouraged and discouraged by the tiniest of changes, knowing it can go either way in the blip of a respirator or the beat of a heart monitor.

The hands that use a computer to connect me to you now minister to my Mother as I will her with all I have to stay with us awhile longer.

We have more work still to do.

Come on down, Dale!
June 10, 2007

It was 1965, the summer that LBJ increased troops in Vietnam and signed the Voting Rights Act into law.

"Doctor Zhivago" and "The Sound of Music" filled movie screens, Bob Dylan shocked fans by going electric at the Newport Folk Festival and Michener, Bellow and Hailey had bestsellers.

Television was filled with shows about a talking horse, a family of hillbillies who struck it rich and a housewife who cast spells by twitching her nose.

My husband, 9 at the time, was an ardent fan of "Flipper," while his parents tuned in to "Truth or Consequences," hosted by the relentlessly charming Bob Barker.

That summer, the McBrides took a California vacation to Marine World, where "Truth or Consequences" was filming. They didn't get good seats but did have a good view of the swimming tank.

Bob Barker chose two contestants at random, then scanned the crowd for a third.

"Hey, how about you up there in the red shirt, smoking a pipe?"

Back then, my father-in-law Dale was in full pursuit of his lifelong love affair with style. His closet still is filled with white pants, belts, shoes and shirts that look like some crazed impressionist painter's rejects, threads that have caused my conservative husband to cringe through the years.

By golly, it paid off that day.

An usher ran up the steps and shoved a microphone in front of Dale.

"Where are you from?" Bob asked.

"Oklahoma," Dale replied.

"Are you one of those Oklahoma oilmen?" Bob asked.

"No," Dale said, "but I work for an oil company."

"Well, Dale, have you got so much of that Oklahoma oil money that you don't want to make any money today?"

"No," Dale answered, "I would like to make some money today."

"Well," Bob said, "come on down!"

They put Dale and the five other contestants in Gay '90s bathing suits, a striped sight to behold, I'm sure.

"When I saw a boat tied up to the other side of the pool, I knew I was going to get wet," Dale said.

The two teams of three learned the first team to pull the boat from the center of the pool to the edge would split $150 and take home a Ronson electric shaver and a pen and pencil set.

"Of course, the first time we pulled on the rope, the boat tipped over," Dale said. "But I was a good swimmer, as were the other two guys, so we won."

At 1965 prices, Dale's share of the loot — $50 — was enough to pay for the gas to and from California.

Back home, he was a celebrity as coworkers gathered to watch the show and kids got out of school so they could watch.

While Dale was pleased to meet Bob Barker, my husband was awed that his father swam in Flipper's pool.

When Barker appears on his last "The Price is Right" show (to be broadcast Friday), my father-in-law will be watching, remembering the summer he stood side by side with a celebrity.

It also was the summer of the Watts riots, and there's a great story about Dale, a lack of parking spaces and a fire truck, but that's for another day.

Mom

Aug. 5, 2007

At 3 a.m., false illumination surrounds me.

In my mother's intensive care room, it bounces from a fluorescent tube, accented by a bank of lights on the monitors I have watched so carefully for weeks that even when I close my eyes I still see them.

Vibrating monitor lights accompany the constant beeps of alarms that relentlessly remind me of the fragility of her heart, lungs and kidneys.

When the alarms fall momentarily silent and Mother falls into deep sleep, I buzz the steel CVICU doors open and make the slow trek down the tiled floor hallways.

Each forward movement is an effort. The fatigue is visceral, a combination of anxiety, heightened alertness and lack of sleep.

The yellow cast of the parking lot light illuminates my car, easy to spot in the deserted lot. I stop, keys dangling from clenched fingers, wishing that I could, just for this night, hand them to someone else and slip into the passenger seat.

Laying my head against the wheel, I weep for my mother, for the fear and suffering she endures, held captive on a respirator and fed through a stomach tube.

I weep for the loneliness she's battled the last decade of her life. For what could have been. Should have been.

I weep with my own fear that the years she should have left will be taken from her.

I make the familiar drive across town to the motel, slipping between wilted sheets to get a few hours of sleep. The last thing I do before closing my eyes is check the battery on my cell phone, placed within fingertip's reach.

As my mother's advocate, in an Arkansas hospital, I have been hyper vigilant, making decisions about her care as I do my best to navigate through a constant series of crises.

Although I am in touch with my family, at most moments there is neither the time nor the luxury to abdicate that responsibility. No one to ask, "What should I do? How do I know what is best?"

In those moments, we can do one of two things. We can run away, or we can deal with it. In the past, I'd done my share of running. Now, I was exactly where I wanted to be, at my mother's side, but on that lonely June morning, my reserve was depleted.

It's been seven weeks since Mother died, around 3 a.m. on Father's Day.

Each night, as I prepare for bed, I pick up my cell phone and stare at the buttons, reluctant to turn off what has been my lifeline to her.

During those first weeks after her death, I felt lost in my own home. What was I to do now if not tend to and protect my mother?

My therapist, my family and my friends tell me: "Jane, you did everything you could. You couldn't have saved her."

"I know that," I say, lying.

"If only I had talked her out of having the surgery at that hospital," I think. "If only I had insisted on calling in a specialist 24 hours before I did. If only I hadn't believed them when they said she was better and left her to go back to work. If only, if only ..."

I will pass through this grief in time. I understand, and accept, that I can't jump over it, go around it, or dig under it.

So I keep walking.

Orphan Annie
Sept. 2, 2007

Things are so nice around the house these days.

The wide expanses of the beautiful new wood floors in the kitchen and dining room are spot and streak-free, gleaming like burnished copper where the light falls.

The living room looks better than it has in a long time. The couch and loveseat are freshly vacuumed and no threat to guests who, like me, have a closet full of black clothes.

In the bedroom, the coverlet lies flat and unwrinkled, the three rows of pillows plumped and undisturbed.

The antique parlor sofa in the bedroom is cleared of rumpled blankets and the floor no longer is an obstacle course.

All the doors in the house are flung open wide, letting light dance from room to room as the sun moves from the back of the house to the front.

During the past 16 years, I can't remember when the house ever looked better — or when the sight of it hurt worse.

I would trade this tidy place in a heartbeat for a home where the furniture is covered in white hair and the floor littered and streaked with grass and dirt. I'd gladly trade that pristine bed for one with pillows pushed into a jumbled pile and with a rumpled hollow in the center, still warm from a 35-pound lump of love.

My husband would be willing to be awakened at least twice during the night, and I'd be more than happy to close the doors each morning, extra tightly to keep the escape artist contained.

We'd be absolutely fine with stepping over water and food bowls and picking up the pieces of discarded kibble scattered about. I would gladly mop the floors, knowing they would be soiled again within the hour by four muddy feet scrambling for traction and sliding toward the cabinet with the treat jar — if it meant I had my Annie back.

For 16 years, she has been my shadow, her wise, all-seeing brown eyes following my every move.

She has taken hundreds of naps with her head against my chest, breathing in tandem, opening her eyes once in a while to make sure I was still there and that all was well.

She greeted me with devotion and gratitude every time I walked through the door since the day someone tossed her over our fence and into my heart.

When I had breast cancer surgery three years ago this week, she crawled up on the bed and stretched out between me and the mattress' edge, refusing to leave me no matter how strongly my husband, afraid she might inadvertently hurt me, scolded her.

I know that your dog is probably the smartest, most loving, well-behaved, loyal, protective, joy-filled dog on earth.

My Orphan Annie carries that honor in heaven.

Ellie is doing fine

Feb. 3, 2008

Judging by the calls, emails and conversations around town, pet lovers out there are put out that I haven't written a follow-up column on our new family member.

The question always is the same: "How's Ellie?"

Ellie is fine, and thanks so much for asking.

After the death of our beloved Annie a few months back, we decided we would take our time rescuing another dog from the shelter.

Ellie had other ideas.

When we spotted her in a rain-swollen ditch one cold night in December, she crawled cautiously to us. One look in her fear-filled but hopeful amber eyes was all it took.

After verifying she was a stray, we took her in. She was so wary we had to carry her in the house. She went immediately to Annie's bed, curled up and slept for hours.

For the first few weeks, she battled parasites that turned her digestive system into a bloody mess. We battled her distrust.

One night, Joel reached down to unbuckle his belt to get undressed. She cowered in the corner, averting her eyes and curling into the smallest ball she could manage.

Ellie weighed around 30 pounds and her ribs stuck out. She couldn't get enough to eat. It took weeks before she decided that yes, there would be more food coming on a regular basis.

No matter how hungry she was, she never showed food aggression. I could cover her food with my hand and she'd wait. She did, however, make a couple of counter-top raids on a loaf of bread.

Under our vet's care, Ellie's distinctive red merle coat grew shiny and soft.

She loves everyone. When someone new visits, we warn them if they sit on the couch she will hurl herself in their lap and kiss them until they beg for mercy.

Ellie now is 40 pounds of pure energy. She greets us with the same joy each night as she did the first time we came home from work after "abandoning" her.

She adores our grandchildren, especially Jordan, our serious, tender-hearted, deep thinker.

When my sister stayed with us during the arduous two-week trial of the drunk driver who hit and killed her 36-year-old daughter, Ellie stuck to her side and refused to leave. Each night, she'd jump in bed with Gloria and curl up while Gloria spent some time with her thoughts.

"She's just what I needed," Gloria told my husband when she left.

Now that her Aunt Gloria is gone, Ellie occasionally jumps on the guest bed and lies quietly for a while, then comes back to us.

She's a keeper.

Siblings celebrate special events
Feb.17, 2008

It's not every day that your daughter turns 40.

Then again, it's not every day that your son proposes to his girlfriend on stage in front of 100-plus people.

Leave it to my two to combine the duo of momentous occasions.

On Feb. 8, two days before her official birthday, my gregarious firstborn threw herself — and 150 or so close friends — one spectacular party.

Like her, it was rollicking good fun done up with panache.

I wish you could have seen her. The party's theme was "decades," with guests encouraged to dress up in their finest '60s and '70s attire. She was stunning, decked out in a minidress, white go-go boots and hair as "big" as her legs are long.

Her brother was a howlingly funny sight, shirt unbuttoned almost to the waist, showing off his gaudy necklace, white patent belt and a truly hideous goatee and mutton chop sideburns.

His girlfriend was definitely the more attractive Brady of the bunch, her long dark hair in dog tails.

Just before time for the band to go on, Steph took the microphone and handed it to Chris, who said he wanted to toast his sister on her birthday. But before that . . .

He knelt on one knee, pulled out a ring box and prepared to pop the question. Before he could get the whole sentence out, Sheila said, "Yes!"

It was a glorious night. His generous sister, who was in on the surprise, was thrilled to share her evening with him.

What could be better, she said, than watching her brother ask the woman he loved to marry him?

At age 40, Stephanie has built a good life for herself. She has become comfortable, and quite content, with her life a single mother. She is competent, confident, and capable of embracing who she is as the nurturer and leader of her little family.

After so many years of being single that we thought he'd likely never marry again, Chris has found a woman whose sensibilities and sense of humor match his own and who seems to be able to read his thoughts.

We are grateful for both these blessings: a daughter who finds fulfillment in her own accomplishments and a son who has someone with whom he can share the triumphs and trials of his life.

For more years than I can remember I've prayed hard for both my children, asking that they find their own path to peace and joy

Happy Birthday, Stephanie. Congratulations, Chris and Sheila.

A toast to you: May your days be many and your troubles be few. May all God's blessings descend upon you. May peace be within you, may your heart be strong. May you find what you're seeking wherever you roam.

Every soul needs its motorcycle
June 8, 2008

Straddling a motorcycle the color of a robin's egg, the girl in jeans and a T-shirt leaned forward to kiss her lover.

Their bodies touched lightly, her hands reaching for him in the way of those who cannot bear to be parted.

I remember that girl.

Twenty-seven years ago, I was that girl.

I fell in love with a man who has loved motorcycles much longer than he has loved me.

He began riding bikes when he was 13. He bought his first one for $270, paying for it with a paper route. Three bikes later, he had his pride and joy, a KZ 900 with a custom paint job.

We rode that bike everywhere. One of our favorite stops was a friend's tiny neighborhood bar where we'd shoot pool.

When we bought our first house, the bike had to go. We used the money for a down payment.

Joel missed the bike terribly. Four years later, he bought a bright red, sleek Kawasaki Eliminator, a poor substitute for the KZ 900. It wasn't comfortable for a passenger and the lean lines begged for speed, even for the most careful and experienced biker I know. Every time Joel left on it, I worried until he pulled back in the driveway.

When the oil industry took a downturn in the 1980s, Joel put the bike up for sale.

"Don't worry," I told him. "You can get another one later."

Responsibilities piled on and the years rolled by. Occasionally, he'd mention a bike.

By that time, the adventurous girl whose arms encircled his waist as they rode country lanes on the back of a bike became bogged down in middle age and the pursuit of security.

About a year ago, I noticed Joel watching bikes as they drove by.

JANE AND JOEL

He'd turn and give me that wounded look, saying, "Vroom, Vroom." He'd tell his friends: "I'm going to get another bike as soon as I get permission."

My husband is a homebody who works hard, doesn't hunt, fish, play golf or hang out in bars. Other than clothes, tools, kitchen and outdoor living gear, his needs are few.

Last week, we drove to the dealership and Joel picked out "Annie," a beautiful, pearl white cruiser the color of the dog we lost last year.

"I'm not buying this bike unless you bless it," he told me.

By the time I met Joel at 33, my spirit had been battered. Day by day, he repaired it with his love, faith and support. I am a writer because he made me believe I could do it.

"You love riding," I told him. "It feeds your spirit, the way writing feeds mine. In our relationship, I want to help lift your spirit, not break it."

Am I worried about a 52-year-old biker in the midst of a world full of crazy drivers? Yes. But as I told him when he said he didn't want to ride if it filled me with fear, I won't live like that; I have to learn to let go.

We're taking a photograph of us on the new bike, in the same pose as the original one, so I can remember the girl I used to be and be reminded how much I love the man who still takes me riding.

Keeping secrets
June 15, 2008

Ten years ago, I would have done almost anything to keep from writing a Father's Day story, from mumbling excuses about workload to taking an avoidance vacation.

My story is not unique. The plotline is as old as humanity: woman in bad marriage falls in love with another man, has an affair, gets pregnant, and panic-stricken, takes her husband back to avoid scandal, carrying the secret in silence.

In my case, my mother divorced her husband, married another man (not my father) and moved to Texas from her home in Arkansas, leaving me in the care of my grandmother.

Few secrets can be kept completely. The more closely guarded, the louder the whispered rumors. Like most children of extramarital affairs, I grew up knowing that something wasn't quite right and that it had something to do with me.

Each Mothers and Fathers Day, as I watched classmates craft presents and sign cards for their parents, I was reminded in the most public of ways that I had neither. Well, I had them, but they had chosen a life without me in it.

When I was in my early 40s, my mother, reading a story I wrote about a woman who discovered her father had an affair during World War II that produced a child, decided it was time and told me the truth and about Dad. What a gift.

I met my dad and my two new brothers in 1991. We spent time getting to know each other, and those conversations filled in the missing pieces of my history — and my heart.

That Easter, I received a card signed simply, Love, Dad. It was the first time I had seen that word written on something meant for me.

When my editor offered me this column, I delayed its debut so the first one would run on Fathers Day, 1992.

It became one of my favorite holidays. Each year, I sent him two cards.

I lost Dad unexpectedly five years after I met him. It was a cruel blow, but I reminded myself that Mother could have gone to her grave with her secret.

For the past couple of weeks, I've been talking with exceptional men for a Father's Day article on stay-at-home dads. It was a joy to get to know them, witness their devotion and share their stories with readers.

Mothers — and fathers — if you have a secret like my mother did, please think about breaking your silence. Time lost cannot be regained.

I lost my mother one year ago this week.

She died on Father's Day.

Perfectly Imperfect

July 13, 2008

Gator got married last week.

Ron Franscell was my editor for four years and his fiancee Mary became my friend. As any gator will, Ron snapped at me a few times (OK, a lot of times) and made me a better writer for it.

Thursday, at Mary's luncheon, I watched her soak up each moment. I swear this woman must have begun planning her wedding the day she was born.

Mary is as sentimental as she is organized. Everything connected with her wedding was carefully chosen for its meaning.

"I wish you could have seen her at the luncheon," I told Ron on Friday night as we sat in their backyard filled with family and friends, "she was so in her element . . ."

"Being worshiped?" Ron smiled.

Waiting 39 years for the right man will do that to a girl.

As you would expect from a newspaperman/novelist and a teacher/writer, it was a weekend of stories.

Some of them:

Mary's best friend packed her gift in the same bag Mary had given her at her bridal shower almost 20 years before, stuffed with the same confetti.

The groom's cake was an old-fashioned manual typewriter, complete with white letters and ribbon. Ron cut it with a pica pole (a metal ruler that measures picas, or type size.)

The bride's wedding cake topper was the same one that graced Mary's grandparents' cake.

Mary wore a beautiful crystal necklace, given to her by her future mother-in-law, who inherited it from her mother.

The dress was gorgeous, as was Mary in it. Ron cut quite a dashing figure, even when he did his best leg-swinging, pelvic-thrusting Elvis dance at the reception (Please, God, let the videographer have caught that.)

The week before the wedding, I had called Mary, who showed the first sign of nerves and was, I swear, trying to apologize for it.

"You're getting married in a week, for heaven's sake."

"I am. So it's normal to be a little nervous, right?"

"Mary, I can promise you this. The wedding will not be perfect. Something will go wrong. Someone will forget something important, or something will break at the last minute. But I also promise you this: It will be absolutely perfect because you are marrying the man of your dreams, surrounded by people you love and who love you."

The rain held off during the ceremony, held outside under ancient oak trees, but the heavens opened just as everyone was preparing to eat.

Mary didn't get to dance her first dance on the wooden floor on the hillside, but the covered porch made a fine substitute.

Rain shorted out the thousands of tiny lights sprinkled among the huge oak trees on the grounds, but the lights that remained cast gentles circles in the moonlight.

Mary's mother could not be at the wedding because of Alzheimer's disease, but as he walked down the aisle, Ron placed a rose in her chair — and her presence was felt as they played a tape of her singing "The Wedding Song" recorded at a family wedding many years before.

So what's a few slightly imperfect moments scattered among so many perfect ones?

As the dry cleaner said when Mary showed her a four-inch deep band of mud on the hem of her wedding gown, "It shows that you danced."

Being heard – and healed
Oct. 12, 2008

In those first few days and weeks after a mammogram finds cancer, women listen as experts do all the talking, throwing around words like sentinel node, mastectomy and other terms they could have gone a lifetime without hearing.

The best medical folks listen, too, patiently answering questions, explaining options and inviting the patient to take control of treatment options and post-recovery care.

Healing begins when a woman is heard.

Every year brings new options. When I was diagnosed with breast cancer four years ago, radiation therapy attacked the tumor, and the rest of the breast with it. Now, in some cases, radiation can be confined to a much smaller area, decreasing the possible collateral harm done to the heart and lungs.

Hope keeps breast cancer patients going when they feel most helpless.

Leading that hope is the battle to perfect screening and treatment options. In Southeast Texas, we are blessed to have the Julie Rogers Gift of Life Program and the American Cancer Society joining the fight, from providing free mammograms to helping fit women with prosthesis.

Women who opt not to have reconstructive surgery appreciate those soft, silicone molds like the one the American Cancer Society provides that help fill in sunken spots and make a bra fit again. At my house, where I tend to start shedding clothes and tossing them aside as soon as I get home, my husband is used to hearing me ask the next morning as I get dressed, "Have you seen my boobie?'

A few months ago, I slipped across the street to the Beaumont fire museum and signed my name on the bright pink fire truck of the Guardians of the Ribbon, five firefighters traveling to raise funds and honor those with cancer.

I ran a hand across the hot pink fire hose, admiring the paint job.

"Why don't you sign it," a fireman said. "I hand-painted it."

I picked up the pen and wrote: "My grandmother, Ruby Johnson Nowlin, claimed by cancer."

As I left, the firefighter yelled across the street, "I'll never forget you. Know why?"

I shook my head.

"You're the first one to sign the hose."

We can only dream of the day when some woman will be the last.

Thanksgiving
Nov. 23, 2008

When I think of my family, traditional is not the first word that comes to mind.

We are a rather convoluted and, in my opinion, interesting bunch.

When it came to affairs of the heart, Mom got around. Between her and Dad, I have 10 siblings.

We chose a variety of careers. On my maternal side, we are, or have been, in insurance and government service, journalism, transportation, bookselling, law enforcement, refinery work and the medical field.

We strongly endorse the merits of individualism.

We are Buddhist, Christian, agnostic and undeclareds, but we all believe in the power of the human spirit and the right to pursue our own paths.

We thrive on literature, board games, off-beat humor, conversation . . . and adventurous cuisine.

Until Thanksgiving rolls around.

Then, you'd think we had been brought up in a Norman Rockwell home.

We want our turkey and dressing, mashed potatoes, yams, green bean casserole, baked corn and pie.

Occasionally, we will throw in an exotic side dish, and we might serve flavored herbal tea, but when we start the round of e-mails on who's bringing what, it becomes clear that you do not mess with tradition.

Even though the conversation around the dinner table might range from politics to sports, from growing older to the merits of a particular philosophy, when it comes to turkey day food, we are as predictable as post-Thanksgiving indigestion.

I find this comforting.

As much as I love trying new dishes, on holidays I need the buttery flavor of potatoes and sweet yams, the tartness of cranberry sauce and the hint of sage in cornbread dressing. Such traditional flavors make me feel grounded. They remind me that I belong to a place and people who are my past — and my future.

Trying to convince my ultra-finicky grandsons to carry on the tradition could prove to be quite a challenge, however.

Ham, turkey and mashed potatoes? Fine. But they'll have nothing to do with dressing, yams or pumpkin pie.

My only hope is that, like their mother, they will develop a more adventurous palate later in life.

Until then, we'll work on board games, literature and conversation. True to their genes, they've already got the humor down pat.

That's a great place to start.

Wild wedding was perfect storm
May 3, 2009

There will be no more weddings in our family. As Chief Mom of the Family Supreme Court, that's my ruling.

It's so exhausting.

I thought the wedding stage in our family was long past. My 41-year-old daughter is a single mom who is quite content answering to no one but herself — and her children, of course. Children never stop asking, you know. At some point, you decide to stop answering.

My 38-year-old son has been single so long that I figured he'd decided marriage was not for him. While I knew he often was lonely, he didn't show any signs of becoming one half of a married-filing-jointly family again.

Along came Sheila.

Their relationship began as friends — always a good choice. They knew each other for years before they took it to the next level.

A year ago, at his sister's 40th birthday party (and with her full endorsement), he lured Sheila to the band's stage with a phony reason and then, shocking her speechless, knelt on one knee and proposed.

Thank goodness she said "Yes."

"No" would have been a real party-killer.

They had a year to plan for their small, simple spring wedding. About two months ago, things started jumping. As the parents of the groom, our role was blessedly limited. We did what we were told, when we were told.

Sheila chose spring colors: yellow and lavender. Hubby Joel bought a white shirt, black pants and yellow tie, and I bought a yellow blouse and black pants. Joel was quite handsome; I looked like a giant daffodil.

About two weeks before the wedding, Sheila came down with a case of "OMG, I'm getting married!" We carefully chose our words, uttering soothing phrases at every opportunity and promising her things would

CHRIS AND HIS WIFE, SHEILA

be perfect.

We knew better, but hey, you don't mention last-minute calamities to a jittery bride-to-be who was GOING TO HAVE THE PERFECT WEDDING AND THAT'S ALL THERE IS TO IT!

When I'd ask my son, Chris, some questions that would be useful for those involved, like, "Why do your nephews need one purple shirt and one white. Are they in the wedding?" he'd sigh and say, "Mom, I don't know. I just run errands."

At the rehearsal, Sheila put us through our paces. Once she saw that we all had our roles down, she began to relax and had a great time at the rehearsal dinner.

The day of the wedding, it rained. No, make that poured. Thunder-booming, lightning-illuminating, sheets-of-water-falling rain.

A half-hour before it was to start, Chris, who was decidedly pale except for the dark circles under his eyes, told me his computer was unable to copy the wedding music they'd spent many hours working on. They went to a back-up plan.

Fifteen minutes before the wedding march was to begin, they realized the pianist hadn't shown up — and the church had no CD.

Back-up plan No. 2.

Ten minutes before start time, Chris walked out. It seems they had left the marriage license at home.

Three minutes before walk-down-the-aisle-time, he rushed in, big brown eyes glazed over, marriage license in hand.

The wedding was sweet and perfect in all the ways that matter. The people they loved and who loved them were there to share in their commitment to each other.

Chris was handsome and Sheila was lovely and no rain could dampen their joy.

The next morning, they left for a quiet, relaxing honeymoon at the lake. I breathed a sigh of relief, knowing there finally would be some peace for them.

And then I heard about the big fishing tournament that weekend.

Thank God it was a different lake.

Sheila, welcome to our crazy family and all that means — including being written about in this column, by the way. I'm sure Chris must have mentioned it at some point. Like maybe after the ink on the license had dried.

Open hearts
May 10, 2009

The last 12 months have been a big year in our family.

As a wife, I watched my husband make the difficult decision to leave the company he has loved for 23 years. Although he wasn't looking for a new job, having been loyal to growing the company all those years, a larger company he respected and trusted made him an offer he couldn't turn down.

Moving on was even harder than he expected. He'd made numerous friends through the years, watching people come and go while he remained. He'd also made lots of friends among his clients. He genuinely liked and respected his bosses, who gave their blessing and then gave him a going-away party to show their appreciation for all those years of hard work.

As a mom, I watched my daughter step out to take a demanding job with a big company that promised fewer hours and a better life financially, but one with its own high-level challenges.

Stephanie settled into the job, which she loves and gives thanks for every day, and then found the house of her dreams after a six-year search.

She sold the home she and the boys had made so many memories in, attacked the huge job of getting her old house ready to sell, then packed up a lifetime of accumulations for the move.

Leaving was even harder than she expected, she said through tears. Now, she wakes up smiling each morning as the sun floods the house through a wall of windows.

On my daughter's 40th birthday, I watched my son, who has been single for a lot of years now, propose to the woman whose friendship had deepened into love.

On April 18, Chris married Sheila, who promised to be there for him, and he for her, until death chooses to separate them.

Walking away from the thing we know, for the thing we don't can be frightening, especially in this uncertain world. Whether it's a job, a home, or a life into which we've settled with some comfort, it requires an act of courage — and faith.

Courage to take a chance on something you hope enriches your life, and faith that it all will work out for good.

My wish for you is that you open your heart to all the possibilities life brings your way, whether anticipated — or entirely unexpected.